COOKING IN A
HALOGEN OVEN

COOKING IN A
HALOGEN OVEN

HOW TO MAKE THE MOST OF YOUR COOKER WITH OVER 60
DELICIOUS RECIPES AND 300 STEP-BY-STEP PHOTOGRAPHS

JENNIE SHAPTER

LORENZ BOOKS

This edition is published by Lorenz Books, an imprint of Anness Publishing Ltd, Blaby Road, Wigston, Leicestershire LE18 4SE; info@anness.com

www.lorenzbooks.com;
www.annesspublishing.com

If you like the images in this book and would like to investigate using them for publishing, promotions or advertising, please visit www.practicalpictures.com for more information.

Publisher: Joanna Lorenz
Editorial Director: Helen Sudell
Executive Editor: Joanne Rippin
Photographer: Bay Hippisley
Props Stylist: Liz Hippisley
Food Stylist: Jennie Shapter
Designer: Adelle Morris
Production Controller: Bessie Bai

ETHICAL TRADING POLICY
At Anness Publishing we believe that business should be conducted in an ethical and ecologically sustainable way, with respect for the environment and a proper regard to the replacement of the natural resources we employ.
As a publisher, we use a lot of wood pulp in high-quality paper for printing, and that wood commonly comes from spruce trees. We are therefore currently growing more than 750,000 trees in three Scottish forest plantations: Berrymoss (130 hectares/320 acres), West Touxhill (125 hectares/305 acres) and Deveron Forest (75 hectares/185 acres). The forests we manage contain more than 3.5 times the number of trees employed each year in making paper for the books we manufacture.

Because of this ongoing ecological investment programme, you, as our customer, can have the pleasure and reassurance of knowing that a tree is being cultivated on your behalf to naturally replace the materials used to make the book you are holding.
Our forestry programme is run in accordance with the UK Woodland Assurance Scheme (UKWAS) and will be certified by the internationally recognized Forest Stewardship Council (FSC). The FSC is a non-government organization dedicated to promoting responsible management of the world's forests. Certification ensures forests are managed in an environmentally sustainable and socially responsible way. For further information, go to www.annesspublishing.com/trees

© Anness Publishing Ltd 2011

A CIP catalogue record for this book is available from the British Library.

NOTES
Bracketed terms are intended for American readers. For all recipes, quantities are given in both metric and imperial measures and, where appropriate, in standard cups and spoons. Follow one set of measures, but not a mixture, because they are not interchangeable. Standard spoon and cup measures are level. 1 tsp = 5ml, 1 tbsp = 15ml, 1 cup = 250ml/8fl oz. Australian standard tablespoons are 20ml. Australian readers should use 3 tsp in place of 1 tbsp for measuring small quantities. American pints are 16fl oz/ 2 cups. American readers should use 20fl oz/2.5 cups in place of 1 pint when measuring liquids.
Oven temperatures in this book are for halogen ovens only. Ovens vary, so you should check with your manufacturer's instruction book for guidance.
Medium (US large) eggs are used unless otherwise stated.
The nutritional analysis given for each recipe is calculated per portion (i.e. serving or item), unless otherwise stated. If the recipe gives a range, such as Serves 4–6, then the nutritional analysis will be for the smaller portion size, i.e. 6 servings. The analysis does not include optional ingredients, such as salt added to taste.

PUBLISHER'S NOTE
Although the advice and information in this book are believed to be accurate and true at the time of going to press, neither the authors nor the publisher can accept any legal responsibility or liability for any errors or omissions that may have been made nor for any inaccuracies nor for any loss, harm or injury that comes about from following instructions or advice in this book.

The Publishers would like to thank the following companies for supplying halogen ovens for testing and photography: JML Direct Ltd (www.jmldirect.com), Andrew James UK Ltd (www.andrewjamesworldwide.com).

Contents

Introduction

Cooking using a halogen oven is not so different from a conventional oven, it is just faster. This book helps you to get to know your oven and understand the differences between the models available. Read through the introductory pages of this book alongside your halogen oven instruction manual before you begin to cook.

All the recipes have been developed specifically for a halogen oven and have been tested in a range of halogen ovens to give you as much useful information as possible. Timings for each halogen oven will vary depending on the manufacturer, so always double-check any timings given in this book with a similar recipe in your oven manual. The cooking times given in the recipes in this book often include a range of times, to cover the differences between one oven and another. Always check the food being cooked after the shortest time given, so that it doesn't over-cook.

Before you start, it is useful to take a couple of basic foods, such as toast and bacon, and check your cooking times against those given on pages 14–17. This will give you some idea of how the timings for your oven fit with the timings given in this book. For example, if toast only takes 1 minute in an oven preheated to 250°C/482°F, it means your oven cooks more quickly

than another oven that takes 3 minutes to make the toast; or, your oven may be halfway between these timings. For the faster ovens, over-browning is more likely to happen, so where a recipe suggests using an extension ring, this is likely to be necessary for your oven.

Many of the recipes serve four, but in some, for instance where only two fish will fit on one rack, the recipe serves two. You will find that as you become more experienced, you can cook four fish; two on the top rack, and two on the bottom, changing them as needed so that all are cooked at the same time.

Often specific dishes to use when cooking are suggested in the recipes. Timings and results will differ if, for example, you use a different diameter dish, or you use an ovenproof glass dish when a cast iron dish has been recommended. In these cases you will learn how to adjust the timings as you get to know your oven. The cooking times will also vary depending on whether food has just come out of the refrigerator or is at room temperature. With cuts of meat and fish, the weight may be the same but they may be thicker or thinner pieces than those used for testing in this book. Check food, as you would with a conventional oven, to make sure it is cooked, and don't rely on the cooking times given.

Above: Test temperature and timings of your oven by toasting bread and seeing how long it takes to brown.

For most recipes, it is recommended to preheat the oven. This is not essential, but the oven only takes a short while to preheat, and this will slightly reduce the cooking time. Check with your manual for recommended preheat times. If none are given, watch to see when the halogen oven light turns off; this means it has reached the set temperature.

The important thing is to experiment with different recipes; very soon you will realize what an exciting addition your halogen oven is to the kitchen.

Right: The halogen oven is great for a quick snack or a complete meal for four.

Below: The halogen oven is ideal for steak, as it cooks quickly on the outside.

Below: For many recipes you need to preheat the oven.

Below: A halogen oven is able to cook several things at the same time.

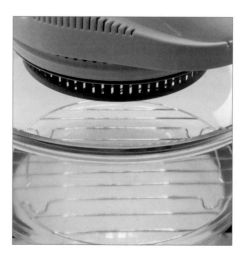

What is a Halogen Oven?

Thermal Transmission
The infrared element in the halogen oven lid heats up almost instantly. It emits heat waves, which directly penetrate the food. This browns and crisps the food as well as sealing in the juices and flavours of meat and fish in particular.

Heat Transmission
This is the same as a conventional oven in that it uses conduction to heat and cook the food.

Convection
A fan in the lid of the oven circulates the hot air around the food to give more even cooking and browning. This reduces the need to turn food or move its position during cooking.

Advantages of a Halogen Oven
The halogen oven cooks most foods more quickly than a conventional oven. Depending on what you are cooking it can be up to 40% quicker, though in general it is around 20% faster. This obviously saves on power, as does the fact that it will run from a wall socket, which uses less electricity than a wired-in conventional oven.

The halogen oven is cleaner to cook in because it uses very little oil or fat, so there is less splattering. An important advantage of the halogen oven is that as less fat is used to cook meat and fish, or to roast potatoes, for instance, the finished food is better for you.

A halogen oven is a compact tabletop cooker powered by electricity. It is a completely different way of cooking compared to that of a conventional oven because it uses a halogen light source to produce energy, which then cooks the food. The halogen oven plugs into an ordinary electrical wall socket, so there is no need for any sort of heavy-duty permanent wiring. As you can just plug it in, it makes it extremely portable, so the oven can be moved to different areas of the kitchen to suit or used in a holiday home or caravan provided the correct power source is available.

Unlike a microwave oven, the halogen oven will brown and crisp foods, just like a conventional oven. It will also cook on more than one level so you can prepare a whole meal. It can be used as a stand-alone cooker or to complement your existing equipment.

The halogen heat source is in the lid of the cooker, which sits on a large glass

Above: A 12-litre halogen oven, with a black baffle plate.

bowl where all the cooking takes place. The halogen light source produces infrared waves, which will grill, roast, bake or steam food. The halogen oven works using three different methods of cooking; thermal transmission, heat transmission and convection.

Below: Black baffle plate.

Below: Chrome baffle plate.

Above: A 10-litre oven with a flat baffle.

Above: An oven with a fixed handle.

Choosing an Oven

All halogen ovens work in a similar way, with a halogen heat source in the lid. The temperature gauge and timer are also located in the lid. Some cookers have the temperature in Centigrade (°C) only, while others have dual Centigrade (°C) and Fahrenheit (°F) settings.

A handle on the top of the lid opens the oven. Lots of models also use this handle as a safety switch, and only when the handle is folded back and down will the oven operate. Other models have a pushdown handle, which is secured by pressing a button to re-set the safety switch and activate the oven. You may prefer one type to another, so try both and see which is most comfortable to operate.

Halogen ovens are available in different powers (wattage) and sizes. They vary from 1100 to 1400 watts. The smaller ones tend to be 1100 watts, while the larger ones vary between 1200 and 1400 watts. The higher wattage ovens cook slightly faster, but there is also some variance between models of the same wattage.

One of the main factors that seem to determine how quickly the larger ovens cook is the design of the baffle plate, which covers the halogen light source in the lid. Some models have a slotted plate, while others have a plate with small holes in like a colander. The latter seem to give a gentler browning than the slotted variety as the plate dissipates the energy more. Both have their plus points. When you want to quickly sear cuts of meat, the former is best; if you are intending to bake cakes, desserts, pastry or cook larger dishes,

Below: Baking bread, desserts and cakes is easy in a halogen.

the latter is probably best. Both will provide good results; you simply have to employ slightly different cooking techniques to achieve the best results.

As far as size is concerned, you need to consider how much space you have available to either place the oven on the work surface or store it in a cupboard. As well as space for the cooker, you need space next to it to place the lid rack, as the lid cannot be put straight down on the work surface when hot.

Consider also how many people you want to cook for and whether the oven is being used to cook for one or two, or for larger family meals.

Most ovens come with a self-cleaning function, which means you can simply add hot soapy water to the glass bowl, set the timer, and the debris on the bowl will be loosened.

Another point to consider is how much you want to spend. Does the price include any extras, such as an extension ring, a rack for the lid or round baking trays? If not, the extra cost of these may make a cheaper model more expensive. Work out which of these features are important to you and look at all the models that are available before you make any purchasing decisions.

Oven Components and Equipment

The halogen oven consists of a large glass bowl, a plastic base to lift it off the work surface, and a lid containing the heating element and controls.

The Glass Bowl

This is used either directly or with racks where food or heatproof cooking containers are placed. The size of the glass bowl varies between models, but for the majority of models it is around 30–33cm/12–13in wide.

The Stand

The bowl becomes very hot during use so it is essential that the stand, which has two handles to make moving it easy, is always used. The stand should always be placed on a level, stable, heatproof surface. Do not place it near the edge of the work surface.

The Lid

The removable lid houses the halogen element on the underside, the temperature and timer dials on the top and the mains cable. The mains cable is permanently wired in on most models, but on some it is plugged in at the back of the lid, so can be removed for easier storage. The halogen element is housed on the underside of the lid, behind a baffle plate. Never immerse this in water.

There are two control switches. The temperature dial is controlled by a thermostat that ranges from 0°C/32°F to 250°C/482°F. The second dial is a timer, which can be set from 0 to 60 minutes.

Below: Stand for holding a hot lid.

Above: Oven lid and control switches.

There are two lights – a power source which illuminates when the oven is powered and a thermostat light which cycles on and off while the oven is in use, as the temperature is regulated.

The top of the lid also has a handle for lifting it on and off and a lock which, when pushed down, acts as a safety switch, which will allow the halogen oven to operate. Some models have a separate button to press, which operates the safety switch.

Lid Stand

This is used to hold the lid when removed from the oven. The lid should never be placed directly on the work surface as it will burn the surface.

Steel Racks

Halogen ovens usually come supplied with two cooking racks – one low and one high rack. These can be used to place food directly on, or to support dishes and trays. You can use both at the same time to provide two cooking levels. Food on the high rack will cook more quickly than food on the low rack.

OPTIONAL ITEMS

Some ovens will come with the following extras, others you may have to purchase separately.

Extension Ring

Sometimes an extension ring is included in the price of the oven, but if not, it is worth buying. This fits on top of the glass bowl, moving the heat source further away from the food, so that larger food items can be cooked. It is also useful for avoiding over-browning before the food is cooked all the way through. The use of the extension ring is suggested to achieve the best results in a number of the recipes in this book.

Baking and Steamer Trays

A round baking tray is extremely useful and comes as standard with some models. If not, it is worth buying one as an optional extra, as most baking pans will not fit in the halogen oven. You can also use the removable metal base from a loose-bottomed cake tin or flan tin. Some ovens come with a round steamer tray. This is useful when you are cooking foil parcels of vegetables for steaming, and is also good for heating up pre-cooked foods such as croissants, pastries, pizzas and pies.

Below: Steamer rack.

Below: Extension ring.

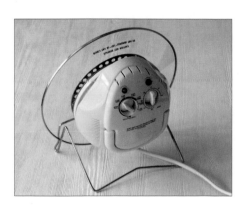

Skewers and Tongs

Your oven may come with skewers that are purpose-made to fit within the oven. Tongs are really useful for lifting out hot trays that don't leave much space for oven gloves around the edge.

EQUIPMENT AND COOKWARE

You can use any utensils, casserole dishes, ovenproof bowls, roasting pans etc, that you would use in a traditional oven, providing they will fit into your halogen oven and leave a small gap around the edges, so that the hot air can circulate properly.

Casserole Dishes

Clear heatproof dishes are useful as you can see what is happening during cooking. Cast iron casserole dishes are ideal if you are searing meat, or browning vegetables such as onions, before making a casserole, as the heat of the cast iron cooks the food faster. While you can cook directly in the glass bowl, cooking in a casserole dish allows you to place it on the low rack so the hot air can circulate, resulting in a faster and more even cooking process. A casserole dish of around 20–23cm/8–9in is probably the most useful size.

If a recipe suggests covering the dish with a lid, make sure the handle is metal. If it is a heatproof non-metallic handle, cover the handle with foil, shiny side outside, to deflect the heat. If the casserole lid touches or nearly touches the lid, add an extension ring.

Bakeware

Use the same flan tins (pans), tart tins and cake tins, as you would do in a conventional oven. For muffins and cupcakes, you will need to source a 6-hole muffin/cupcake tin as most 12-hole tins are too large.

Foil

You will need foil to make parcels when steaming or cooking vegetables. It can be used to protect food from over-browning on the top or burning, as the halogen oven quickly browns food. You can also use it to wrap around a rack to make a temporary tray. Whenever foil is used, make sure it is secure and cannot lift upwards on to the halogen element

Above: Dishes suitable for a halogen oven include Pyrex, cast iron and non-stick.

in the lid when the fan is operating. If used instead of a lid for a casserole dish, you might wish to put the dull side on the outside, as this will reflect less infrared energy.

Timer

As the timer on the cooker continues to count down even when the lid is removed, to stir the food, for example, the time left on the machine can then be misleading, so a separate timer is useful. Set a separate timer for each step of the recipe, so it reminds you when to stir, turn or check if cooked.

Below: Tongs for lifting out trays.

Below: Oven gloves and timer.

Below: Foil parcel for steaming.

How to Use a Halogen Oven

It is important to read the instruction manual for your oven properly. Any information given in this book covers a range of halogen ovens, while a manual is specific to your model.

1 Place the oven on a stable, heatproof surface near to a mains power source. Ensure there is sufficient space alongside for the lid rack, and that the power cord is not touching anything or hanging over the work surface.

2 Place the low or high rack in the oven, according to the type of food you wish to cook. For foods that are likely to drip juices, place a round baking tray in the base of the oven to catch them.

3 Place the food on the rack or racks (unless you are preheating first) then place the glass lid on top, making sure the timer and temperature selectors are set to 0. Ensure that the lid sits inside the inner rim of the bowl. If preheating the oven, put the food in when the halogen light goes out.

4 Plug the oven into the mains supply. Set the temperature by turning the dial in a clockwise direction. Then set the cooking timer by turning clockwise from 0 to 60 minutes. Never turn it the other way as it may damage the oven.

Above: Make sure you have sufficient space around your plugged-in oven.

5 Push the handle down on the lid. On some models, the handle must be flat down behind the controls for the oven to operate; on others, the handle is pushed down and there is a separate button, which must be pressed.

6 Once the oven is switched on, the halogen light will glow. The green light and halogen lamp will cycle on and off to show the temperature is being regulated. There will also be a noise from the fan that circulates the hot air.

7 At the end of the cooking time, the timer will ring and the cooker will switch off. If you are following a recipe where you need to remove the lid while food is cooking, remember the timer is still

counting down so you will need to adjust the timer accordingly. Always watch your oven while in use, and keep a check on the food inside. Foods cook quickly and can easily overcook or burn.

8 Remove the food using long-handled tongs, or use oven gloves or oven tongs to remove a container. Be careful, as the sides of the glass bowl will be very hot, as will the racks.

Getting The Best From Your Halogen Oven
• Leave room for the air to circulate around the food for even cooking. Do not stack food on top of each other or against the sides of the glass bowl.
• When using both racks at the same time, place the food that takes the longest to cook on the base first, then add food on the upper rack as required.
• Cover dishes or add an extension ring to prevent over-browning.
• Do not add light foods such as herbs on top of dishes as they will lift off with the air movement from the fan. If using, make sure they are tucked in beneath the food in the dish.
• When the food has finished cooking, turn the temperature right down to about 100°C/212°F to keep it hot. Remove food to prevent moisture building up in the oven.

Safety Points
• A halogen oven is for adult use only. Never leave the oven unattended while in use. Keep an eye on food being cooked; check the food regularly. Food can quickly burn.
• Do not touch the bowl or lid during use as they become very hot.
• Make sure there is sufficient space around the appliance for ventilation, to allow heat and steam to escape. Do not use near or below combustible materials such as curtains.
• Ensure food does not come into contact with the heating element in

the lid. If using foil as a lid make sure it is securely fixed, otherwise it may detach with the airflow and be sucked up into the heating element.
• If wrapping foods in foil or baking parchment, make sure they are weighted down so they cannot lift with the air movement.
• Don't turn the timer backwards; it could damage the oven.
• Never cover the cooker in any way when in use. Make sure the electrical cord does not hang over the edge of the work surface or touch hot surfaces.
• If preheating a dish in the oven, do not

leave unattended. Be ready to add food once the oven has heated, and take care, as the dish will be hot.
• Always use oven gloves or gauntlets and remember the sides of the glass bowl will be hot.
• In the event of a fire, do not remove the lid. Unplug at the mains and cover the appliance with suitable fireproof material.
• Never immerse the lid in water.
• Do not operate the halogen oven with other appliances from the same power socket.
• Don't move the oven when in use.

What to Cook in a Halogen Oven

You can cook most foods in a halogen oven that you would normally cook, roast or bake in a conventional oven or grill (broiler). Unlike a microwave oven, the halogen oven will brown food, producing crispy browned toppings on cakes and cookies, succulent roast meat and roasted vegetables.

Defrosting

Some ovens have a defrost or thaw setting, which is useful for small items. Refer to your instruction manual for specific guidelines. You may be able to cook frozen foods straight from the freezer. Always make sure food is thoroughly cooked before serving.

Meat and Fish

You can cook traditional meat roasts of lamb, pork, beef or poultry and add potatoes or other vegetables alongside to cook. You can also grill meat such as steaks, kebabs, burgers, etc. Fish can be grilled, baked, roasted or steamed.

Vegetables

Roasting vegetables works very well. To cook vegetables that would normally be boiled, you can steam them in foil parcels instead. These do however take

Above: Roasting is the best way to cook vegetables in a halogen oven.

a while to cook, especially root vegetables. You can shorten the roasting time of root vegetables by parboiling them first, while the oven is preheating, in much the same way as you might do with a conventional oven.

Cakes, Breads, and Pastries

All types of baking can be done in the halogen oven. Hints and tips on how to get the best results can be found with each recipe. To reheat bread rolls or garlic bread, wrap in foil and heat for a few minutes at 200°C/392°F.

Advantages
- The halogen oven uses less energy and cooks more quickly.
- It uses less fat for roasting, and the rack allows any fat to drain away from the food to the base of the oven and so can be discarded.
- Meat and fish remain very succulent and moist.

Points to Consider
- The size of the oven may limit the amount of food you can cook. You may have to use other cooking sources to cook a complete meal.
- Foods that need to rehydrate, like pasta or rice, need pre-cooking.
- Vegetables take a while to cook, so you may need to parboil them, or start cooking the vegetables before adding the meat or fish.
- The fan, which circulates the hot air, is quite strong so the halogen oven is not ideal for liquid dishes such as soups. For flan fillings, you may need to add a dispersing baffle to protect the centre of the filling.

Below: Fish cooks well in a halogen oven, as the insides stay tender.

Below: Halogen ovens are great for all in one meals, like this casserole.

Below: Desserts, cakes and even breads cook beautifully in a halogen oven.

Cooking Times and Methods

Given below are cooking times for a selection of everyday foods you are likely to want to cook in the halogen oven. These times are general guidelines only, as the times will vary according to the thickness, shape and temperature of the food before cooking. Always keep a close eye on what you are cooking.

MEAT
The halogen oven is ideal for grilling steak, bacon, burgers and sausages as the meat cooks quickly and browns well. Fat also drains away, so it is a healthier way to cook.

Bacon and Sausages
Cook bacon at 200°C/392°F on the high rack. Don't overlap the bacon. Cook for 5–9 minutes or until the fat is crispy.

Place 4 sausages (about 225g/8oz total weight) on a shallow round baking tray. Place the high rack in the oven and put the baking tray on top. Cook at 200°C/392°F for 8 minutes, then turn and cook for a further 4–7 minutes, until browned and the juices run clear.

Beef or Lamb Steaks
Brush 175g/6oz beef or lamb steaks with sunflower oil and season with ground black pepper. Place the high rack in the oven and place the steak on

Above and right: The best breakfast sandwich ever, with deliciously crispy bacon, cooked in a halogen oven.

top. Cook at 200°C/392°F for 8–15 minutes, depending on how rare you like your steak. Turn over after 4–8 minutes.

Chicken Breast
Place up to 4 skinless chicken breast fillets on a shallow round baking tray. Brush with sunflower oil and season with salt and ground black pepper. Place the high rack in the oven and put the chicken on top. Cook at 200°C/392°F for 12–17 minutes, until tender and the juices run clear. You can also use skin-on chicken if you prefer.

VEGETABLES
The halogen oven roasts vegetables very well, and will even steam them, if you need it to, in portion-sized amounts. Often, however, parboiling vegetables is recommended, as in the halogen oven they actually take longer to cook than meat or fish.

Roast Potatoes
Peel 225g/8oz potatoes and cut each into even-sized pieces. Place in a pan of boiling water and parboil for 5 minutes. Drain well. Meanwhile, place the low rack in the oven and preheat to 200°C/392°F. Toss the potatoes in 10ml/2 tsp sunflower oil to coat thoroughly. Place on a shallow round

Below: Chicken breast fillets cook well, with or without the skin.

Below: These lamb steaks have been marinated before cooking.

Below: Sausages cook to golden-brown perfection in a halogen.

Above: Perfectly cooked baked potatoes take about an hour in the halogen.

Below: Potatoes roast more quickly in a halogen oven and need less fat.

Above: It is healthier to cook chips or fries in a halogen oven.

baking tray. Cook for 17–22 minutes, until the potatoes are tender and golden, turning 2–3 times. If you like, you could double the quantity, but you may need to add a couple of minutes to the cooking time.

Baked Potatoes
Cooking potatoes this way is quicker than a conventional oven, and gives a crispier skin than a microwave. Place

Frozen Oven Chips
It's easy to cook or reheat frozen food such as oven chips in your halogen oven. To cook some spicy oven chips, turn the oven on to 220°C/425°F. Place the chips in a single layer on a baking tray and sprinkle them with your favourite spices, such as chilli, paprika or cumin, then cook for 16–20 minutes until the chips are golden.

the low rack in the oven and preheat to 200°C/392°F. Scrub the potatoes and, while still damp, sprinkle with salt. Prick or score the skin. Wrap the potatoes in foil, shiny-side innermost. Place the wrapped potatoes on the rack and cook for 40 minutes. Remove the foil and cook for a further 10–15 minutes, until the flesh is tender and the outsides are slightly browned.

Chips/Fries
Peel 225g/8oz potatoes and cut into 1cm/1⁄2in thick chips. Toss in sunflower oil to coat thoroughly. Place the chips on a shallow round baking tray, season with salt, and put on the low rack. Cook at 220°C/425°F for 25–30 minutes, until tender and golden.

Broccoli
Place 125g/41⁄4oz small broccoli florets in a single layer on a large sheet of foil. Add 30ml/2 tbsp water. Fold over the foil and seal into a flat parcel. Place on the low rack. Set the oven temperature to 200°C/392°F and cook for 15–25 minutes, until just tender.

Cauliflower
Place 125g/41⁄2oz small cauliflower florets on a large sheet of foil. Add 30ml/2 tbsp water. Fold over the foil and seal into a flat parcel. Place on the low

rack. Set the oven temperature to 200°C/392°F and cook for 18–25 minutes, until just tender.

Green Beans
Place 100g/3oz green beans on a sheet of foil. Add 45ml/3 tbsp water. Fold and seal into a flat parcel. Set the oven to 200°C/392°F and cook for 15–18 minutes on the low rack, until tender.

Carrots
Slice 125g/41⁄4oz carrots about 5mm/ 1⁄4in thick (if thicker they take longer to cook), in a single layer on a piece of foil.

Below: Vegetables such as broccoli are best cooked in portion-sized batches.

Above: Carrots need to be cooked thinly sliced and wrapped in foil.

Above: Any vegetable you would grill or fry cooks well in the halogen oven.

Roasted Peppers and Onion

The halogen oven excels at roasting vegetables as well as meat. Preheat the oven to 200°C/392°F. Place sliced red and yellow (bell) peppers in a baking tray with segments of onion. Toss in olive oil, season, and roast in the oven on the top rack for 10–15 minutes, until soft. Add a few cloves of garlic after 5–7 minutes. You may need to move the baking tray to the lower rack if over-browning before tender. When cooked, remove from the oven, add a little balsamic vinegar and serve.

Add 15ml/1 tbsp water and 15ml/1 tbsp lemon juice. Fold over the foil and seal into a flat parcel. Place on the low rack. Set the oven temperature to 200°C/392°F and cook for 25–30 minutes, until just tender.

Parsnips

Place the low rack in the oven. Preheat the oven to 200°C/392°F. Peel 125–225g/4–8oz young parsnips. Cut them in half widthways, then cut the thick ends lengthways into 2–4 even-sized pieces. Toss the pieces in

Below: Parsnips, like potatoes, roast very well in the halogen oven.

sunflower oil and place on a shallow, round baking tray. Roast for 17–22 minutes, until tender and golden, turning after 10 minutes.

Mushrooms

Place the low rack in the oven and preheat to 200°C/392°F. Place the mushrooms on a flat try, brush with oil and cook for 7–10 minutes, until tender.

Tomatoes

Place the high rack and preheat to 230°C/450°F. Cut two tomatoes in half, dot with butter and season. Place on a round baking tray or foil on the high rack and cook for 3–4 minutes.

Below: Moist and tasty grilled tomatoes.

Above: Eggs don't need any water to be 'boiled' in a halogen oven.

EGGS

Place the low rack in the oven and preheat to 200°C/392°F. Place 2 eggs on the rack and cook for 8–10 minutes for hard-boiled eggs. Plunge the eggs into cold water unless you wish to serve them hot. If you wish to cook soft-boiled

Cheese on Toast

With a halogen oven, cheese on toast is easy. Place the high rack in the oven and preheat to 220°C/425°F. Place slices of French bread in the oven for 1½–2 minutes to toast. Turn the toast over, top with sliced or grated cheese and cook for 1–2 minutes, until the cheese is bubbling.

eggs, then cook for 5–6 minutes. Use tongs or oven gloves to remove the eggs from the oven, as they will be very hot. You may cook up to 6 eggs at a time. Just make sure they are evenly spaced out to allow room for the hot air to circulate.

TOAST

Preheat the halogen oven to 250°C/ 482°F, and add the high rack. Add 1 or 2 slices of toast and cook for 1–3 minutes, turning as necessary. Some ovens come with a toast rack, which will cook several slices of bread at a time.

ADAPTING RECIPES

As with any piece of new equipment, it takes a bit of experimenting to work out how to best use it for the foods you like to eat. Use the recipes in this book as a guideline on how to adapt your own favourite recipes.

The settings on the halogen oven are similar to those of a traditional oven, but remember the cooking times of a halogen oven will be quicker. Use your normal cooking temperature but check food earlier to see if it is cooked. If food in a dish browns or cooks too quickly, move it to the low rack, add an extension ring, reduce the oven temperature or cover the dish with a lid or foil. To ensure food is cooked, check meat with a meat thermometer or pierce it with a fork or skewer to make sure the juices run clear; with cakes, a skewer inserted into the centre of the cooked cake should come out clean.

Vegetables that need liquid or steam to cook are possibly the most difficult food to adapt because they will take longer to cook and often longer than the meat or fish, so you need to start cooking them first. The smaller you cut them the quicker they will cook. However, do not cut them too small or they will lose their texture. Roasting is quicker and more effective than steaming in the halogen oven, and as with a conventional oven, parboiling first will speed up the cooking time.

Care and Cleaning

• Disconnect the halogen oven from the electrical supply when cleaning unless using the self-clean function.
• Do not use abrasive cloths, as this will damage the cooker.
• Clean the glass bowl in hot soapy water or in the dishwasher. Clean the racks in hot soapy water.
• The lid assembly must never be immersed in water. Wipe it down with a soft, damp cloth and a mild detergent solution.
• All Fahrenheit, and most Centigrade, halogen ovens have a self-clean function. After using the oven, you simply remove any food and drain away any fat, then leave the oven to cool, otherwise the bowl may crack when water is added. To clean, just add 2–4cm/1–2in of hot water and a drop of washing-up detergent. Place the lid on the glass bowl and turn the temperature dial to the wash position or to 80°C.
• Push the safety lock handle down. Set the timer for 5–15 minutes. The combination of the swirling motion from the fan, the hot water and washing-up liquid should loosen and clean most stains. The racks may also be left in the oven to soften any stains, which will then easily wash away.
• Once the cleaning process has finished, leave the oven to cool, then pour the water away and thoroughly dry all parts.

Appetizers and Snacks

With a halogen oven, cooking small amounts of food is quick and easy, so that a snack of crostini or some deliciously melting goat's cheese can be whipped up at a moment's notice, and with virtually no clearing up afterwards. If the halogen oven is your only cooking source, you can even create dishes such as filo tarts or falafel for effortless appetizers or an impressive light lunch.

Spicy Baked Prawns

Watch these prawns carefully through the halogen oven's glass lid. Serve as an appetizer for four people, or as a snack for two, with crusty bread to mop up the juices.

Serves 4

20 raw large tiger prawns (jumbo
    shrimp), peeled, heads removed
1 red chilli
2 garlic cloves
30ml/2 tbsp olive oil
60ml/4 tbsp dry white wine
freshly ground black pepper
15ml/1 tbsp chopped fresh flat leaf
    parsley, to garnish
lemon wedges and warm crusty bread,
    to serve

1 Slit each prawn along the back and remove the dark intestinal vein.

2 Cut the chilli in half and remove the seeds, then chop the chilli and garlic and place in a shallow dish. Add 15ml/1 tbsp of the olive oil and the prawns, and toss together to coat the prawns. Cover and chill for 15 minutes.

3 Place the low rack in the oven and place a cast iron gratin dish on top. Preheat the oven to 220°C/425°F. Add the remaining oil to the gratin dish and cook for 1 minute.

4 Add the prawns with the garlic and chilli, and cook for 2 minutes. Turn the prawns over, add the wine and cook for 2–3 minutes, or until the prawns are pink and sizzling. Keep an eye on the prawns to check when they change colour. It is important to make sure they are cooked, but avoid overcooking.

5 Transfer to warm plates or individual dishes. Sprinkle with black pepper and the flat leaf parsley. Add a lemon wedge and serve immediately with warm crusty bread to soak up the juices.

Energy 79kcal/333kJ; Protein 18g; Carbohydrate 0g, of which sugars 0g; Fat 1g, of which saturates 0g; Cholesterol 195mg; Calcium 84mg; Fibre 0.2g; Sodium 191mg

Baked Eggs with Salmon and Spinach

Perfect for the halogen oven, this one-dish appetizer takes little time to prepare and minutes to cook. Serve with Granary bread to complement the flavour of the salmon.

Serves 2

knob (pat) of butter, for greasing
25g/1oz baby spinach leaves
50g/2oz smoked salmon trimmings
2 eggs
45ml/3 tbsp single (light) cream
15g/½oz Parmesan cheese, grated
freshly ground black pepper

1 Place the lower rack in the halogen oven and preheat it to 200°C/392°F. Lightly grease two individual oval gratin dishes of approximately 150ml/¼ pint/ ⅔ cup capacity.

2 Divide the spinach leaves and smoked salmon trimmings between the two individual gratin dishes.

3 Using the back of a teaspoon, make a small indent in the centre of each dish and carefully break an egg into each hollow. Pour the single cream over the spinach and salmon.

4 Season with a good sprinkling of black pepper, then add the grated Parmesan cheese over the top of the eggs.

5 Place the dishes into the preheated halogen oven, and bake for 5–6 minutes, or until the eggs have just set. Cook for a couple of minutes longer if you prefer a firmer yolk. Remove from the oven and eat while warm.

Variation Replace the smoked salmon with strips of ham, if you prefer, and use Cheddar cheese instead of Parmesan.

Energy 221kcal/921kJ; Protein 18g; Carbohydrate 1g, of which sugars 1g; Fat 16g, of which saturates 8g; Cholesterol 265mg; Calcium 159mg; Fibre 0.5 g; Sodium 651mg

Chicken Skewers with Peanut Sauce

The ginger, soy sauce and spices in the marinade for these chicken skewers combines beautifully with the slightly piquant peanut dipping sauce to make a tasty appetizer.

3 To make the peanut sauce, heat the oil in a pan, add the shallot, garlic and ginger and cook for 3 minutes.

4 Add the peanut butter, lime juice, chilli powder, coconut milk and 45ml/3 tbsp water to the pan, and bring to the boil stirring all the time. Simmer for 4–5 minutes, stirring occasionally, and then set aside.

5 Place the high rack in the oven and preheat to 200°C/392°F. Thread the marinated chicken pieces on to the skewers, piercing them in a zigzag fashion. Shred the spring onions.

6 Place the skewers on the rack and cook for 4–5 minutes, turn them over and cook for a further 2–3 minutes, until browned and the chicken is cooked.

7 Serve the chicken skewers with the warm peanut sauce, lime wedges and shredded spring onions. They can be served on one large or four individual plates as preferred.

Serves 4

350g/12oz skinless chicken breast fillets
1 shallot, finely chopped
10ml/2 tsp grated fresh root ginger
45ml/3 tbsp light soy sauce
5ml/1 tsp ground coriander
5ml/1 tsp ground cumin
30ml/2 tbsp sunflower oil
spring onions and lime wedges
    (scallions), to serve

For the dipping sauce:
15ml/1 tbsp sunflower oil
2 shallots, finely chopped
1 garlic clove, finely chopped
10ml/2 tsp grated fresh root ginger
100g/3¾oz /scant ½ cup crunchy
    peanut butter
30ml/2 tbsp lime juice
2.5ml/½ tsp hot chilli powder
120ml/4fl oz/½ cup coconut milk

1 Cut the chicken breast lengthways into thin strips about 1cm/½ in wide. Soak 12 15cm/6in wooden skewers in water for 30 minutes, this will prevent them burning in the oven.

2 In a shallow dish mix the shallot, ginger, soy sauce, coriander, cumin and oil together. Add the chicken, toss together, cover and leave in the refrigerator to marinate for 1 hour.

Energy 172kcal/718kJ; Protein 22g; Carbohydrate 2g, of which sugars 2g; Fat 9g, of which saturates 1g; Cholesterol 62mg; Calcium 18mg; Fibre 0.2g; Sodium 855mg

Roasted Pepper and Artichoke Tarts

Filo pastry works really well in a halogen oven, and these pretty little tarts crisp up beautifully. Always preheat the oven when you are cooking with pastry.

Serves 4

1 red (bell) pepper
25g/1oz/2 tbsp butter, melted
3 sheets filo pastry
25g/1oz walnut halves
8 antipasti artichoke quarters in oil
4 stoned (pitted) black olives
5ml/1 tsp chopped fresh oregano
50g/2oz soft blue cheese such as
    Dolcelatte, Gorgonzola or Roquefort
freshly ground black pepper
a few sprigs of watercress or salad
    leaves, to serve, if you wish

5 Add three more layers, arranging each square a quarter of the way around each tin (pan) so the corners of pastry form a pretty star shape. Place the tins on the lower rack of the oven, well spaced, and cook for 2–4 minutes, until light golden.

6 Divide the walnuts, peppers, artichokes, olives and oregano between the four tins. Season with black pepper and crumble the cheese over the top. Bake for 3–5 minutes to melt the cheese. Remove from the tins and serve warm.

1 Cut the red pepper into halves, remove the seeds, and cut into strips. Place on a shallow baking tray.

2 Place the high rack in the oven and preheat the oven to 200°C/392°F. Add the tray of peppers and roast for 5–6 minutes, or until softened. Remove from the oven, reduce to 175°C/347°F, and place the lower rack inside.

3 Brush 4 x 10cm/4in, 2–2.5cm/³⁄₄–1in deep round fluted loose-bottomed tart tins (pans) with butter. With the sheets of filo pastry on top of each other cut into 8 equal rectangles about 12 x 12cm/4¹⁄₂ x 4¹⁄₂in. Brush the top layer with melted butter.

4 Line each tin with a square of filo pastry, pressing it into the sides of the tin, brushing each layer of pastry with melted butter first.

Energy 223kcal/928kJ; Protein 13g; Carbohydrate 6g, of which sugars 3g; Fat 18g, of which saturates 7g; Cholesterol 23mg; Calcium 94mg; Fibre 1.2g; Sodium 300mg

Oven Baked Spanish Omelette Tapas

These squares of Spanish omelette, flavoured with peppers and Serrano ham, are delicious warm or cold. You can prepare them in advance and reheat in the oven before serving.

Serves 4

45ml/3 tbsp sunflower oil
250g/9oz/1 very large potato, peeled
  and thinly sliced
1 onion, thinly sliced
1 red (bell) pepper
6 medium mushrooms
5 eggs, lightly beaten
15ml/1 tbsp chopped fresh flat leaf
  parsley
50g/2oz Serrano ham, or wafer thin
  ham, torn into strips
salt and freshly ground black pepper

1 Place 30ml/2 tbsp oil in a large frying pan, add the potatoes and onion, and cook over a gentle heat for 15 minutes, turning, until the potatoes are almost soft.

2 Cut the pepper in half and cut into strips. Slice the mushrooms. Add the pepper and mushrooms to the frying pan and cook for 5 minutes.

3 In a large bowl, mix together the eggs, parsley and seasoning. Stir in the ham.

4 Grease a 20cm/8in shallow square cake tin (pan) with the remaining oil. Place the tin on the lower rack in the halogen oven. Set the temperature to 180°C/350°F and heat for 5 minutes.

5 Add the cooked pepper and mushroom mixture to the beaten eggs and ham, and stir gently to mix.

6 Transfer the egg mix to the preheated tin and cook at 180°C/350°F for 13–17 minutes, or until the egg in the centre is just cooked.

7 Leave to stand for 10–15 minutes, then cut into squares and serve warm, or leave to cool completely before cutting into squares and serve cold.

Energy 317kcal/1319kJ; Protein 16g; Carbohydrate 16g, of which sugars 5g; Fat 21g, of which saturates 4g; Cholesterol 290mg; Calcium 66mg; Fibre 2.9 g; Sodium 365mg

Tomato and Brie Crostini

The halogen oven is perfect for this easy-to-make but impressive appetizer of crispy garlic toast topped with succulent tomatoes and Brie. You could also serve this as a quick snack.

Serves 4

175g/6oz vine tomatoes, quartered
2 spring onions (scallions), chopped
5ml/1 tsp dried oregano
30ml/2 tbsp olive oil
30ml/2 tbsp balsamic vinegar
4 slices crusty bread or French bread
1 clove garlic, cut in half
75g/3oz Brie, cut into slices
freshly ground black pepper
rocket (arugula) leaves, to serve

1 Place the tomatoes in a bowl with the spring onions, oregano, 15ml/1 tbsp olive oil and 15ml/1 tbsp balsamic vinegar. Toss together.

2 Place the high rack in the oven and preheat to 250°C/482°F. Arrange the bread slices on the rack, well spaced, and toast for 3–4 minutes until golden.

3 Remove the bread from the oven and turn over, so the slightly browned side is uppermost. Rub the cut garlic lightly over each slice of bread.

4 Arrange the Brie slices and tomatoes on the toasts. Return to the high rack of the oven, and cook at 225°C/437°F for 3–5 minutes, or until the cheese melts and the tomatoes have softened.

5 Sprinkle the crostini with ground black pepper, and serve immediately, with a few rocket leaves drizzled with the remaining oil and vinegar.

Cook's Tip If using French bread, cut diagonally to make the slices of bread larger.

Variation Spread the toast with pesto instead of garlic and try goat's cheese instead of the Brie.

Energy 249kcal/1042kJ; Protein 8g; Carbohydrate 24g, of which sugars 3g; Fat 14g, of which saturates 5g; Cholesterol 17mg; Calcium 106mg; Fibre 2.6g; Sodium 355mg

Falafel Wraps with Tzatziki

These falafel cook very well in the halogen oven, as it crisps up the outsides while leaving the middles perfectly cooked. Warm the flatbreads in the oven at the same time, for a very convenient and delicious lunch, served with a refreshing mint and yogurt tzatziki.

Serves 4

400g/14oz can chickpeas, well drained
1 onion, grated
2 garlic cloves, crushed
8 sprigs fresh coriander (cilantro),
  chopped
4 sprigs fresh parsley, chopped
2.5ml/½ tsp salt
seasoned flour, for shaping
4 x 23–25cm/9–10in flatbread or wraps
large handful mixed salad leaves
3 tomatoes, chopped
4 spring onions (scallions), chopped
1 red chilli, finely chopped, optional

For the tzatziki:
¼ cucumber, seeded and very finely
  diced or grated
30ml/2 tbsp fresh mint, chopped
1 small garlic clove, crushed
175g/6oz natural (plain) yogurt

1 Place the chickpeas, onion, garlic, coriander, parsley and salt in a food processor and process to a fairly smooth but slightly grainy purée.

2 Divide the purée into 12 equal pieces, and using floured hands, shape them into balls and flatten them slightly.

Variation For spicy falafel, add 5ml/1 tsp each of ground chilli and cumin to the mix in step 1.

3 Place the falafel on an oiled tray that will fit in the oven, leaving a space between each one.

4 Seal the wraps in a sheet of foil and place on the lower rack in the oven, then add the higher rack and place the falafel tray on top.

5 Set the halogen oven to 200°C/392°F and cook the falafel for 5–6 minutes, while the wraps heat gently below.

6 Place the cucumber, mint, garlic and yogurt for the tzatziki in a bowl and mix together. Cover and chill until needed.

7 Remove the tray of falafel from the oven and flip over so both sides brown. Return to the oven for 5–6 minutes more.

8 Remove the wraps and falafel from the oven. Divide the leaves, tomatoes and spring onions between the wraps. Add the chilli, if using. Top with falafel and a little tzatziki. Roll up and serve immediately, together with the remaining tzatziki in a bowl.

Energy 254kcal/1080kJ; Protein 11g; Carbohydrate 51g, of which sugars 6g; Fat 2g, of which saturates 0g; Cholesterol 0mg; Calcium 89mg; Fibre 5.1; Sodium 411mg

Baked Goat's Cheese Salad

A quick and easy appetizer, which is perfect for summertime eating. Make sure you use goat's cheese with a rind so that as the cheese melts, it maintains its shape.

2 Put the olive oil, vinegar, mustard and honey in a bowl. Arrange the salad leaves on four individual serving plates.

3 Place the top rack in the oven and place the baking tray with the cheese on it. Set the oven to 200°C/392°F. Depending on your oven, cook for 3–6 minutes, until soft and golden.

4 Meanwhile, whisk together the salad dressing ingredients in the bowl. When the cheese is cooked, remove from the oven. Lift the cheese with a spatula on to the salad leaves.

5 Sprinkle over the walnuts and basil leaves. Drizzle with the dressing and serve at once with crusty bread.

Serves 4

300g/11oz traditional goat's cheese with
 rind, cut into 4 slices
90ml/6 tbsp olive oil
45ml/3 tbsp white wine vinegar
7.5ml/1½ tsp wholegrain mustard
5ml/1 tsp clear honey
75g/3oz mixed salad leaves
50g/2oz walnut halves, coarsely
 chopped
12 small basil leaves
crusty bread, to serve

1 Place the cheese slices, spaced well apart, on a round oiled tray that will fit inside your halogen oven.

Variation This recipe can also be made using 2 x 150g/5oz goat's cheese logs, each cut into 6 slices. They will take the same time to cook as the larger slices above.

Energy 492kcal/2031kJ; Protein 14g; Carbohydrate 4g, of which sugars 4g; Fat 47g, of which saturates 14g; Cholesterol 53mg; Calcium 294mg; Fibre 14.1g; Sodium 746mg

Spicy Potato Wedges with Chive Dip

A perfect appetizer when entertaining friends for a relaxed midweek meal. Just serve a plate of wedges with the dip and a glass or two of chilled white wine.

Serves 4

4 x 125g/5oz medium potatoes
30ml/2 tbsp sunflower oil
15ml/1 tbsp fresh orange juice
2.5ml/½ tsp chilli powder
15ml/1 tbsp Dijon mustard
2.5ml/½ tsp salt

For the chive dip:
150ml/5fl oz/⅔ cup crème fraîche
30ml/2 tbsp chopped fresh chives

1 Scrub the potatoes and pat dry with kitchen paper. Cut each into six lengthways. Place in a large bowl.

2 Mix together the oil, orange juice, chilli powder, mustard and salt and pour over the potatoes. Toss to coat evenly.

3 Place the low rack in the oven and preheat to 220°C/425°F. Arrange the potatoes on a round baking tray and cook in the oven for 15–25 minutes, stirring after 15 minutes. If your oven browns quickly, stir after 10 minutes.

4 Meanwhile, mix the crème fraîche and chives together to make the dip.

5 Check the potatoes to see if golden and tender, and when they are cooked, transfer them to a warm serving plate and serve with the bowl of chive dip. If serving these wedges as finger food, provide napkins to wipe your hands.

Variation Instead of chive dip you can also serve the wedges with garlic mayonnaise, or spicy tomato sauce.

Energy 307kcal/1277kJ; Protein 4g; Carbohydrate 23g, of which sugars 2g; Fat 23g, of which saturates 11g; Cholesterol 42mg; Calcium 32mg; Fibre 2g; Sodium 325mg

Fish Dishes

For the best results, fish needs to be cooked quickly for it to retain its flavour and texture, so a halogen oven is perfect for most fish recipes. Don't forget you can cook most types of fish very easily indeed by simply adding butter, salt and pepper and quickly grilling it in the oven. A fillet of fish will take around 10 minutes, but check it every few minutes so you can remove it from the heat the second it is ready. The recipes in this chapter are easy to prepare and quick to cook, and will become firm favourites for family suppers or when entertaining.

Fish Cakes

Crispy-coated fish cakes are always popular. As these are baked in the halogen oven rather than fried in oil, they are a much healthier alternative to traditional fish cakes.

Serves 4

275g/10oz skinless haddock fillets
350g/12oz/4 cups cooked potatoes,
    mashed
15g/½oz/1 tbsp butter, softened
30ml/2 tbsp fresh parsley, chopped
2 spring onions (scallions), chopped
1–2 eggs, lightly beaten
plain (all-purpose) flour, for shaping
50g/2oz/1 cup fresh white breadcrumbs
15ml/1 tbsp sunflower oil, optional
salt and ground black pepper
crispy mixed leaf salad and tartare
    sauce, to serve

1 Place the fish in a pan, cover with cold water, bring to the boil, then lower the heat and poach gently for 10–15 minutes, until the fish is just cooked.

2 Drain the fish and flake the fillets, discarding any bones. Place in a bowl, add the mashed potatoes, butter, chopped parsley and spring onions, and season with salt and pepper.

3 Add a little of the beaten egg (about 1–2 tsp) to bind the mixture together. It should have a firm texture.

4 Divide the mixture evenly into 8, then with floured hands, shape into flat round cakes. Place the remaining beaten egg and breadcrumbs on separate plates.

5 Brush or dip the fish cakes in the egg, then toss in the breadcrumbs to coat all over. Arrange on a plate and chill in the refrigerator for 30 minutes to firm up.

6 Place the low rack in the oven and preheat the oven to 200°C/392°F. Place the fish cakes on an oiled round baking tray, spaced evenly apart.

7 Cook the fish cakes for 12–15 minutes, until cooked through and golden. Turn them over once after 6–8 minutes (and drizzle with sunflower oil for a moister crumb, if you like).

8 If your oven browns quickly and the crumbs start to brown after the first couple of minutes, insert an extension ring. Serve the cooked fish cakes immediately with a crispy salad and tartare sauce.

Energy 288kcal/1215kJ; Protein 21g; Carbohydrate 29g, of which sugars 1g; Fat 20g, of which saturates 11g; Cholesterol 237mg; Calcium 269mg; Fibre 6.1g; Sodium 1794mg

Fish Pie

This delicious fish pie, made with smoked haddock, prawns, hard-boiled eggs, spinach and peas, is a meal in itself. The eggs can be cooked in the halogen oven first, if you wish.

Serves 3–4

400g/14oz smoked haddock
500ml/17fl oz/generous 2 cups milk
65g/2½oz/5 tbsp butter
1 onion, chopped
40g/1½oz/⅓ cup plain (all-purpose) flour
75g/3oz large cooked peeled prawns
 (shrimp)
75g/3oz baby spinach leaves
100g/3½oz/scant 1 cup frozen peas
2 hard-boiled eggs, shelled and
 quartered (see page 17)
675g/1½lb/3 large potatoes, boiled until
 soft and drained
salt and ground black pepper

1 Place the haddock in a shallow pan, pour over 450ml/¾ pint/scant 2 cups of the milk and bring to the boil. Reduce the heat and simmer for 10–15 minutes, until the fish is tender.

2 Melt 50g/2oz/4 tbsp butter in a pan, add the onion and cook for 5 minutes, until softened. Stir in the flour and cook for 30 seconds. Remove from the heat.

3 Strain the milk from the fish and gradually stir the milk into the butter, onion and flour mixture. Return to the heat and gently bring to the boil, stirring constantly, until thickened.

4 Flake the fish and add it to the sauce with the prawns, spinach and peas. Cook over gentle heat for 2–3 minutes, until hot. Stir in the eggs.

5 Melt the remaining 15g/½oz/1 tbsp of the butter and mash well with the cooked potatoes and the remaining milk. Season with salt and pepper to taste. Place the low rack in the oven and preheat the oven to 180°C/350°F.

6 Transfer the filling to a 20cm/8in square ovenproof dish and top with the potato mixture, covering the filling completely. Bake for 20–25 minutes, until the potato topping has browned. Use an extension ring to stop the potato browning too quickly, if necessary. Serve at once.

Energy 508kcal/2132kJ; Protein 37g; Carbohydrate 48g, of which sugars 10g; Fat 9.7g, of which saturates 8.2g; Cholesterol 2mg; Calcium 29mg; Fibre 3.1 g; Sodium 150mg

Poached Salmon Parcels

By cooking the salmon fillets in paper parcels, it seals all the flavours inside the package and keeps the fish succulent. Serve with new potatoes and sugar snap peas.

3 Place the low rack in the halogen oven and preheat to 200°C/392°F. Place two lines of cucumber slices along the centre of each sheet of baking parchment, slightly longer than the salmon fillets. Place a salmon fillet on top of each and season with salt and pepper.

4 Slice the butter into six slices and place three on top of each salmon fillet. Sprinkle over the lime zest and juice. Lift up the opposite sides of the paper and fold together, then seal the ends. Place on a round baking tray, spaced apart.

5 Cook for 17–20 minutes, until the fish is tender and cooked through. Serve the parcels immediately on warmed serving plates, leaving each person to open their own parcel.

Serves 2

50g/2oz/¼ cup butter, at room
   temperature
15ml/1 tbsp green peppercorns in brine,
   (drained) and chopped
10ml/2 tsp fresh dill, chopped
5cm/2in piece cucumber, thinly sliced
2 salmon fillets (with skin on), each
   about 150g/5oz
finely grated zest and juice of 1 lime
salt and ground black pepper

1 Cut two baking parchment squares, each measuring about 30cm/12in. Use a little of the butter to grease the paper.

2 Beat the remaining butter in a bowl until pale and fluffy. Mix in the peppercorns and dill. Transfer to a small sheet of baking parchment and shape into a roll. Wrap the paper around the butter and twist the ends. Freeze for 20 minutes.

Variation The cucumber slices can be replaced with thin slices of gherkin, if preferred. Cut the gherkins diagonally to produce larger slices.

Energy 460kcal/1904kJ; Protein 31g; Carbohydrate 1g, of which sugars 1g; Fat 37g, of which saturates 16g; Cholesterol 128mg; Calcium 49mg; Fibre 0.2 g; Sodium 614mg

Marinated Salmon Steaks

Fish cooks well in the halogen oven, staying tender and moist. Lemon grass, ginger, soy sauce and fresh chilli give a rich flavour to these salmon steaks. Serve with noodles.

Serves 4

1 stalk lemon grass, thinly sliced
2.5cm/1in piece fresh root ginger, peeled and grated
1 fresh red chilli, seeded and chopped
finely grated zest and juice of 1 lemon
30ml/2 tbsp dark soy sauce
30ml/2 tbsp olive oil
4 salmon steaks, each about 150g/5oz
90ml/6 tbsp natural (plain) yogurt
45ml/3 tbsp coriander (cilantro), chopped
noodles and pak choi (bok choy),
    to serve

1 Place the lemon grass in a shallow non-metallic dish with the ginger, chilli, lemon zest and juice, soy sauce and olive oil, and mix together.

2 Turn the salmon in the marinade to coat. Cover and chill in the refrigerator for 30 minutes. Place the low rack in the halogen oven and heat to 200°C/392°F.

3 Place the salmon on an oiled shallow round baking tray and cook for 7 minutes.

4 Meanwhile, mix together the yogurt and 30ml/2 tbsp of the coriander in a small bowl. Cover and chill in the refrigerator.

5 Remove the salmon from the oven, gently turn the steaks over, baste with the marinade and return to the oven to cook for a further 5–8 minutes, until cooked.

6 Serve the salmon on warmed plates garnished with coriander. Add a spoonful of the coriander yogurt, and serve with noodles and pak choi.

Variation Add 5ml/1 tsp tamarind paste to the marinade.

Energy 369kcal/1509kJ; Protein 32g; Carbohydrate 3g, of which sugars 2g; Fat 25g, of which saturates 4g; Cholesterol 77mg; Calcium 82mg; Fibre 0g; Sodium 517mg

Savoury Crusted Trout Fillets

This fish recipe is so quick and easy to cook in the halogen oven. The crusty topping and the horseradish dressing can be made in advance, so it only takes minutes to put together. Serve with fresh asparagus and new potatoes for a light summer meal.

Serves 2

40g/1½oz day-old white bread slices, crusts removed
1 garlic clove
1 small handful fresh flat-leaf parsley
1 small handful fresh basil leaves
2.5ml/½ tsp paprika
finely grated zest and juice of ½ lemon
30–45ml/2–3 tbsp olive oil
2 trout fillets (with skin on), each about 175g/6oz in weight
250ml/8fl oz/1 cup crème fraîche
15ml/1 tbsp horseradish sauce
15ml/1 tbsp fresh flat leaf parsley, chopped
salt and ground black pepper
lemon wedges, to serve

1 Process the bread to fine crumbs, add the garlic, parsley and basil and process again. Transfer to a bowl and stir in the paprika, salt and pepper, lemon zest and juice, and 15ml/1 tbsp of the olive oil.

2 Line a round baking tray with foil and secure around the edge so that it won't flap in the oven. Lightly oil the foil.

3 Place the trout fillets on the prepared tray and drizzle over the remaining oil. Press a little of the breadcrumb mixture on top of each trout fillet, dividing evenly. Place the low rack in the oven and preheat the oven to 200°C/392°F.

4 Mix the crème fraîche, horseradish and chopped parsley together in a small serving bowl. Set aside.

5 Cook the trout fillets for 8–12 minutes, until the fish is cooked through. Serve at once on warmed plates with lemon wedges and the horseradish dressing.

Energy 963kcal/3992kJ; Protein 40g; Carbohydrate 16g, of which sugars 5g; Fat 83g, of which saturates 39g; Cholesterol 259mg; Calcium 169mg; Fibre 1.5g; Sodium 479mg

Sea Bass with Fennel and Tomatoes

The aniseed flavour of the fennel beautifully complements the subtle taste of the roasted sea bass. This dish is finished with roasted tomatoes and capers, and needs nothing more than some new potatoes or a pile of couscous to complete the meal.

Serves 2

2 sea bass fillets (with skin on), each
   about 125–150g/4½–5oz
30ml/2 tbsp olive oil
1 fennel bulb, thinly sliced
1 red onion, thinly sliced
90m/6 tbsp dry white wine
2 sprigs cherry tomatoes on their vines,
   cut into small bunches
15ml/1 tbsp capers
salt and ground black pepper

1 Slash the skins of the sea bass fillets with a sharp knife. Brush both sides of each fillet with some of the olive oil and season with salt and pepper. Place the low rack in the oven and put a shallow dish large enough to hold the fish on top. Preheat the oven to 200°C/392°F.

2 Meanwhile, heat the remaining oil in a frying pan, add the fennel and fry for about 5 minutes, until beginning to soften. Stir in half of the onions to coat in the oil and mix with the fennel.

3 Transfer the fennel and onions to the preheated dish, pour in the wine and add the sea bass fillets, skin-side uppermost.

4 Cook for 7–8 minutes in the hot oven, until the fish is almost cooked.

5 Open the oven and scatter the cherry tomatoes around the fish, then replace the lid and cook for 2 minutes more. Open the lid again, and sprinkle over the remaining red onion slices, then cook for a further 2–3 minutes.

6 To serve, remove the dish from the oven and sprinkle on the capers. Serve straight from the dish to warmed serving plates, with new potatoes or couscous.

Energy 337kcal/1403kJ; Protein 31g; Carbohydrate 10g, of which sugars 8g; Fat 19g, of which saturates 3g; Cholesterol 120mg; Calcium 251mg; Fibre 1.9g; Sodium 323mg

Lime and Coriander Tuna with Salsa

Fresh tuna bakes extremely well in the halogen oven, especially if marinated first. Fruit-based salsas are good with tuna and it is delicious with this avocado, cucumber and tomato salsa. Serve with some boiled new potatoes or couscous.

3 Peel the mango, cut the flesh from the stone (pit) and dice. Peel, stone (pit) and dice the avocado. Place the diced fruit in a bowl, add the lime juice, spring onions, coriander, olive oil and chilli, and gently toss together. Set aside.

4 Put a shallow round baking tray in the base of the oven to catch any juices. Place the high rack in the oven and preheat the oven to 220°C/425°F.

5 Remove the tuna steaks from the marinade and place on the rack in the oven. Cook for 3 minutes. Turn over, brush with any remaining marinade and cook for a further 1–3 minutes, until the fish is just cooked in the centre. It can be served slightly pink.

6 Lift the tuna steaks on to warmed serving plates, two per plate, placing one slightly overlapping the other. Serve with a little salsa on the side and the lime wedges. Serve with couscous or buttered new potatoes.

Serves 4

4 tuna steaks, about 150g/5oz each
30ml/2 tbsp olive oil
finely grated zest and juice of 1½ limes
1 fresh red chilli, seeded and chopped
15ml/1 tbsp fresh coriander (cilantro), chopped
ground black pepper

For the salsa:
1 ripe mango
1 ripe avocado
juice of ½ lime
3 spring onions (scallions), chopped
15ml/1 tbsp coriander leaves, chopped
15ml/1 tbsp olive oil
½ red chilli, seeded and chopped
lime wedges, to serve

1 Cut each tuna steak in half. Place the olive oil, lime zest and juice, chilli, coriander and some pepper in a shallow dish and mix together. Add the tuna steaks and toss to coat.

2 Cover and marinate in the refrigerator for 30 minutes, or up to 2 hours.

Energy 399kcal/1688kJ; Protein 37g; Carbohydrate 7g, of which sugars 6g; Fat 25g, of which saturates 5g; Cholesterol 42mg; Calcium 38mg; Fibre 1.1 g; Sodium 75mg

Baked Fish with Dill Stuffing

This recipe is equally delicious using fresh herring or mackerel. Make sure you choose fish that will fit on a baking tray in the oven. You may need to curl the fish slightly around the edge of the tray to fit. Serve the fish with a steamed green vegetable, such as broccoli.

Serves 2

15ml/1 tbsp sunflower oil
1 small onion, chopped
50g/2oz/8 mushrooms, chopped
25g/1oz/¼ cup fresh white
   breadcrumbs
10ml/2 tsp French mustard
finely grated zest and juice of 1 lemon
15ml/1 tbsp fresh dill, chopped
1 egg yolk
2 whole herring or small mackerel,
   about 225g/8oz each in weight,
   gutted and cleaned
25g/1oz/¼ cup plain (all-purpose) flour,
   for dusting
25g/1oz/2 tbsp butter
salt and ground black pepper
lemon wedges and a few dill sprigs,
   to serve

4 When the stuffing has cooled slightly, divide it evenly and use it to stuff the cavities of the prepared fish. Dust the fish with flour, cut slashes across one side of each, and transfer to a lightly oiled dish that will fit inside your oven.

5 Dot the butter over the fish and sprinkle over the lemon juice. Cook in the hot oven for 13–16 minutes, until the fish flesh flakes easily. Serve on warmed plates with lemon wedges and dill.

1 First make the stuffing. Heat the sunflower oil in a frying pan, add the onion and fry for about 5 minutes, until softened. Add the mushrooms and cook for 2–3 minutes.

2 Remove from the heat, then stir in the breadcrumbs, mustard, lemon zest, dill and egg yolk. Season well with salt and pepper.

3 Place the low rack in the oven and preheat the oven to 180°C/350°F. Make 3 slashes across one side of each fish.

Energy 622kcal/2586kJ; Protein 36g; Carbohydrate 19g, of which sugars 3g; Fat 45g, of which saturates 14g; Cholesterol 215mg; Calcium 171mg; Fibre 2 g; Sodium 791mg

Cod with Braised Boulangère Potatoes

This is a simple supper dish that can be taken straight from the oven to the table. The potatoes are braised in thyme-laced stock with onions and topped with succulent cod steaks. All it needs to complete the meal is a dish of cooked fresh peas.

Serves 4

1 onion
15ml/1 tbsp sunflower oil
50g/2oz/¼ cup butter
675g/1½lb/4–5 medium potatoes
30ml/2 tbsp fresh thyme leaves
450ml/¾ pint/scant 2 cups hot
   vegetable stock
450g/1lb skinless cod fillet
salt and ground black pepper
30ml/2 tbsp chopped parsley, to garnish

1 Cut the onion in half, then slice it thinly. Heat the sunflower oil in a non-stick frying pan and sauté the onion for 4–5 minutes, until softened.

2 Use a small knob (pat) of the butter to grease a rectangular dish approximately 18 x 23cm/7 x 9in and 1.5–1.75 litres/2½–3 pints/6¼–7½ cups capacity.

3 Peel the potatoes and slice them as thinly as possible with a very sharp knife.

4 Place the low rack in the oven and preheat the oven to 175°C/347°F. Layer half the potatoes in the prepared dish and top with half of the onions. Sprinkle with pepper, a little salt and half of the thyme. Repeat the layers.

5 Pour over the hot stock. Dot half of the remaining butter over the potatoes. Bake for 40–45 minutes, until the potatoes are just tender. Check after 15 minutes; if the potatoes start to over-brown, cover tightly with foil or add an extension ring.

6 Meanwhile, cut the cod fillets into 4 even-sized pieces. Melt the remaining butter in the frying pan and sear the cod to lightly brown on both sides.

7 Remove the oven lid and place the fish on top of the cooked potatoes. Replace the lid, and cook for 3–4 minutes more, until the fish is cooked through. Remove the dish from the oven, garnish with the chopped parsley and serve at once, with some buttered peas.

Energy 270kcal/1136kJ; Protein 25g; Carbohydrate 32g, of which sugars 3g; Fat 5g, of which saturates 1g; Cholesterol 52mg; Calcium 43mg; Fibre 3.4g; Sodium 465mg

Roast Halibut with Red Pesto

Choose halibut steaks that are not too thick as they will cook more quickly and prevent the flesh from drying out. These halibut steaks are finished with a powerful red pesto topping, which keeps the fish moist and tender while it is cooking.

Serves 4

50g/2oz sun-dried tomatoes in oil, drained
1 small garlic clove, chopped
15g/½oz grated Parmesan cheese
8 fresh basil leaves, chopped
25g/1oz pine nuts
30ml/2 tbsp olive oil
30ml/2 tbsp lemon juice
4 halibut steaks, about 150g/5oz each in weight
30ml/2 tbsp sunflower oil
salt and ground black pepper
shredded spring onions, (scallions), to garnish
couscous and spinach, to serve

1 Place the tomatoes, garlic, Parmesan, basil, pine nuts and olive oil in a blender or small food processor. Add seasoning and lemon juice, and process.

2 Season both sides of the halibut steaks with salt and pepper and brush with sunflower oil.

3 Place a round baking tray in the base of the oven to catch any juices. Place the high rack in the oven and preheat the oven to 200°C/392°F.

4 Place the halibut steaks on the high rack and cook for 4 minutes, then turn over and cook for 6–7 minutes more, until the fish is almost cooked.

Variation The red pesto mixture is a versatile topping that can be used to add flavour to any white fish. Try making double quantities and keep it in the refrigerator for 4–5 days.

5 Spread each steak with the red pesto and cook for a further 3–5 minutes, until the halibut is tender and cooked through and the pesto is starting to brown. Serve at once, garnished with shredded spring onion. Serve with couscous and spinach.

Energy 411kcal/1712kJ; Protein 35g; Carbohydrate 1g, of which sugars 1g; Fat 30g, of which saturates 4g; Cholesterol 56mg; Calcium 88mg; Fibre 0g; Sodium 342mg

Meat Dishes

When it comes to cooking meat, the halogen oven offers the best of all worlds. Searing meat is easy, because the halogen oven can reach a high temperature so quickly. The same effect that you get when using a grill (broiler) can be achieved with less mess and fewer cooking odours, and it can even slow-cook or braise for perfect casseroles. Another benefit of a halogen oven is that you can cook a whole course in one go, slow-roasting some vegetables on one layer and then turning up the temperature to add some meat on the top.

Apricot and Sage Stuffed Chicken with Sweet Potato Chips

These chicken fillets are filled with a fruity apricot stuffing before being wrapped in bacon, which helps to keep the chicken succulent. While the chicken is cooking, sweet potato chips can be cooked on the lower layer to provide a tasty accompaniment.

Serves 4

4 x 125g/4¼oz skinless chicken
   breast fillets
4 rashers (strips) back (lean) bacon
550g/1¼lb/2 sweet potatoes
30ml/2 tbsp sunflower oil
150ml/5 fl oz/⅔ cup hot chicken stock
15ml/1 tbsp wholegrain mustard
30ml/2 tbsp single (light) cream
15ml/1 tbsp chopped fresh parsley
green salad, to serve

For the stuffing:
1 onion, finely chopped
15ml/1 tbsp sunflower oil
40g/1½oz soft dried apricots, roughly
   chopped
15ml/1 tbsp chopped fresh sage leaves
25g/1oz/½ cup fresh white breadcrumbs
about 15ml/1 tbsp milk
salt and freshly ground black pepper

1 First make the stuffing. Place the onion and oil in a frying pan and sauté for 5 minutes, or until light golden.

2 Remove the pan from the heat and stir in the chopped apricots, sage, breadcrumbs and seasoning, stirring well so that the breadcrumbs pick up the oil.

3 Transfer the stuffing to a bowl, add sufficient milk to bind the ingredients together, and leave to cool.

4 Make a horizontal cut in each chicken breast and then stuff each breast with a quarter of the apricot and sage stuffing. Press the chicken together to enclose the stuffing.

5 Wrap a rasher of bacon around each breast, making sure that the filling cut is covered, and secure with wooden toothpicks. If necessary, stretch the bacon rashers slightly with the back of a round-bladed knife first before wrapping around the chicken.

6 Place the bacon-wrapped chicken fillets in a shallow ovenproof dish that will fit your oven. Leave a space between each one. Brush the tops of the chicken parcels with a little oil, and set aside.

7 Place the lower rack in the halogen oven and preheat the oven to 200°C/392°F.

8 Peel the sweet potatoes and then cut into chunky chips (French fries). Place in a bowl with the oil and toss to coat thoroughly. Transfer the chips to a shallow round tray or roasting pan that will fit in the oven, and set aside.

9 Pour the hot stock into the chicken dish. Place in the hot oven on the low rack and cook for 5 minutes.

10 Remove the chicken from the oven, and place the sweet potato tray on the lower rack. Add the high rack and place the chicken on it.

11 Cook for 12–15 minutes or until the chicken juices run clear and the sweet potatoes are cooked. You may need to cover the chicken with foil if the bacon starts to over-brown. Secure tightly so that it doesn't lift when the oven fan is operating. If the chicken is cooking faster than the sweet potatoes, swap the two trays around.

12 Transfer the chicken to warmed serving plates. Stir the mustard and cream into the juices in the dish, and heat for 1 minute in the oven. Remove the toothpicks from the chicken.

13 Stir the parsley into the sauce and pour over the chicken. Serve with the sweet potato chips and a green salad.

Energy 482kcal; 2028kJ; Protein 39g; Carbohydrate 40g, of which sugars 14g; Fat 20g, of which saturates 4g; Cholesterol 107mg; Calcium 94mg; Fibre 6.1g; Sodium 986mg

Pot Roast Tarragon Chicken

This is an all-in-one roast chicken dish. The chicken cooks alongside leeks, baby carrots and shallots in a cider and tarragon sauce. Cooking inside a covered casserole dish in the halogen oven means the chicken is extremely moist and tender.

4 Add the sunflower oil, the remaining butter, the leeks, carrots and shallots to the bacon, and cook for 3–4 minutes.

5 Remove the chicken from the tray and place in the casserole dish, arranging the vegetables and bacon around the sides of the chicken.

6 Add the cider, stock, tarragon and bay leaves to the pot. Make sure the vegetables are submerged in the liquid. Gently bring to the boil. Cover tightly with the lid and place in the halogen oven. Use an extension ring, if necessary. Cook for 45–60 minutes, until the chicken juices run clear when pierced.

Serves 4

1 chicken, about 1.2kg/2½lb in weight
40g/1½oz/3 tbsp butter, melted
4 rashers (strips) back (lean) bacon
15ml/1 tbsp sunflower oil
2 leeks, sliced
225g/8oz baby carrots
4 shallots, peeled and left whole
900ml/1½ pints/3¼ cups dry cider
300ml/½ pint/1¼ cups chicken stock
4 fresh tarragon sprigs
2 bay leaves
75ml/2½fl oz/⅓ cup crème fraîche
salt and ground black pepper

1 Place the low rack in the oven and preheat the oven to 200°C/392°F. Place the chicken on a round baking tray.

2 Brush the chicken with melted butter and season well. Place the chicken in the hot oven, and cook for 10–15 minutes, until light golden.

3 Chop the bacon into strips and fry in the oil in a 23–25cm/9–10in casserole dish on the stove until browned.

7 Remove the chicken to a warmed serving dish and leave to rest. Skim any fat from the juices, then stir in the crème fraîche. Cook for 1 minute.

8 Arrange the vegetables around the chicken and pour over a little of the juices. Serve the remainder separately.

Energy 515kcal/2141kJ; Protein 42g; Carbohydrate 7g, of which sugars 6g; Fat 36g, of which saturates 13g; Cholesterol 197mg; Calcium 72mg; Fibre 2g; Sodium 742mg

Roast Vegetable and Chicken Couscous

This dish is a complete meal in itself and needs no accompaniment, so it is ideal for cooking in the halogen oven. If you wish to make this as a vegetarian dish, omit the chicken and stir in some cubes of feta or goat's cheese with the herbs at the end of the cooking time.

Serves 4

½ fennel bulb, thinly sliced
2 carrots, cut into thin sticks
1 red onion, cut into wedges
30ml/2 tbsp olive oil
225g/8oz skinless chicken breast fillets,
  cut into strips
1 small leek, sliced
1 courgette (zucchini), sliced
175g/6oz/1 cup couscous
200ml/7fl oz/scant 1 cup boiling
  vegetable stock
50g/2oz/¼ cup soft dried apricots,
  chopped
15ml/1 tbsp fresh parsley, chopped
15ml/1 tbsp fresh mint, chopped
juice of 1 lemon
salt and ground black pepper

4 Meanwhile, put the couscous in a cast iron casserole dish, pour over the boiling stock and stir gently. Cover the dish and leave to stand.

5 Swap the trays over in the oven and cook for a further 10–12 minutes, stirring the vegetables after 5 minutes, until the chicken is cooked through.

6 Use a fork to fluff up the couscous and then stir in the vegetables and chicken. Stir in the apricots and season with salt and pepper. Cover tightly with the lid.

7 Place on the low rack of the oven and cook for 3–5 minutes, until hot. Remove from the oven, stir in the chopped parsley and mint, add the lemon juice and serve straight away on warmed plates.

1 Place the low rack in the oven and preheat the oven to 200°C/392°F. Place the fennel, carrots and onion on a shallow round baking tray, add 15ml/1 tbsp of the olive oil and toss together.

2 Place the chicken, leek and courgette on a second round baking tray, add the remaining oil and toss together.

3 Place the tray holding the fennel, carrot and onion on the low rack. Add the high rack and place the tray of chicken on top. Cook for 8–10 minutes, until the chicken is starting to brown.

Energy 338/1416kJ; Protein 22g; Carbohydrate 41g, of which sugars 16g; Fat 10g, of which saturates 2g; Cholesterol 39mg; Calcium 115mg; Fibre 10.7g; Sodium 301mg

Duck with Orange Glaze

The halogen oven is an ideal way to cook crispy duck breast fillets – the excess fat just drains away. These are finished with a tangy orange glaze perfumed with cinnamon.

Serves 4

4 duck breast fillets (skin on), each
   about 175g/6oz in weight
grated zest and juice of 2 large oranges
15ml/1 tbsp clear honey
1 cinnamon stick, broken in half
30ml/2 tbsp thick-cut marmalade
salt and ground black pepper
green beans and mashed potato,
   to serve

Cook's Tip Reserve the duck fat and use for roasting potatoes.

1 Score the skin and fat of the duck breast fillets with a sharp knife, making diagonal cuts at 1cm/$^1/_2$ in intervals. Rub both sides with a generous amount of salt and pepper.

2 Place a shallow round baking tray in the base of the oven, then place the low rack on top. Preheat the oven to 200°C/392°F.

3 Put the orange zest and juice in a small pan. Add the honey and cinnamon and bring to the boil, stirring to dissolve the honey. Simmer for 5 minutes.

4 Place the duck breast fillets, skin-side uppermost, on the low rack and cook for 5 minutes, until the skin is golden. Turn over and cook for a further 3–5 minutes, until the meat is just cooked. It can still be pink in the middle.

5 Meanwhile, stir the marmalade into the orange sauce and heat gently to dissolve. Leave to simmer over low heat.

6 Carve the duck breast fillets into slices on the diagonal. Fan out on warmed serving plates and spoon over a little of the orange glaze. Serve with sliced green beans and mashed potatoes.

Energy 296kcal/1245kJ; Protein 35g; Carbohydrate 14g, of which sugars 14g; Fat 11g, of which saturates 4g; Cholesterol 193mg; Calcium 61mg; Fibre 1.5g; Sodium 301mg

Ham and Pasta Bake

Pasta bakes are always sure to please. Perfect for a quick midweek meal, this recipe uses penne pasta, but you could replace it with a shape of your choice.

Serves 4

15ml/1 tbsp sunflower oil
15g/½oz/1 tbsp butter
1 leek, thinly sliced
200g/7oz/2 cups penne pasta
3 eggs
200ml/7fl oz/scant 1 cup milk
100ml/3½fl oz/scant ½ cup single (light)
  cream
10ml/2 tsp wholegrain mustard
15ml/1 tbsp fresh oregano leaves
115g/4oz Gruyère cheese, grated
115g/4oz/1½ cups button (white)
  mushrooms, halved
2 thick slices ham, about 200g/7oz in
  total, cut into strips
25g/1oz/⅓ cup Parmesan cheese,
  grated
salt and ground black pepper
fresh oregano sprigs, to garnish

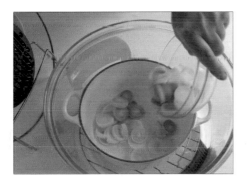

1 Place the low rack in the oven. Place a cast iron casserole or gratin dish on top of the rack and preheat the oven to 200°C/392°F. Add the sunflower oil, butter and leek to the dish and cook for 2–3 minutes.

2 Meanwhile, cook the pasta in a pan of boiling water for 8–10 minutes, or according to the packet instructions. Drain well.

3 In a bowl, beat the eggs, milk and cream together. Add the mustard, oregano, seasoning and half of the Gruyère cheese, and mix.

4 Add the mushrooms to the leeks and cook for 5 minutes, until softened, stirring twice. Stir the pasta into the vegetables. Add the ham and stir through.

5 Pour the egg, cream and cheese mixture over the pasta and vegetables, and gently stir through. Sprinkle over the remaining Gruyère cheese and the Parmesan cheese.

6 Cover with the lid or cover tightly with foil. Reduce the oven temperature to 180°C/350°F, place the dish in the oven, and cook for 25 minutes.

7 Uncover and cook for a further 5–10 minutes, until golden and set. Garnish with a few fresh oregano sprigs sprinkled over and serve immediately.

Energy 566kcal/2372kJ; Protein 31g; Carbohydrate 42g, of which sugars 5g; Fat 32g, of which saturates 15g; Cholesterol 101mg; Calcium 451mg; Fibre 3.8g; Sodium 1044mg

Bacon, Mushroom and Spinach Risotto

Bulgur wheat is used to make this risotto. It is made from cracked wheat and has a fluffy texture and nutty taste. Because the wheat grain is partially processed and cracked it is quick to cook and readily absorbs the flavours of other ingredients.

2 Preheat the oven to 200°C/392°F. Place the bulgur wheat in a bowl, add 450ml/³/₄ pint/scant 2 cups of the hot chicken stock and leave to stand.

3 Add the olive oil, shallots and bacon to the casserole and cook for 6–10 minutes, until the shallots start to brown and the bacon is cooked. Stir after 4 minutes.

4 Add the bulgur wheat and the remaining boiling stock to the casserole dish. Cover and cook for 5 minutes. Drain the mushrooms, reserving the liquor, and finely chop the mushrooms. Add the mushrooms to the casserole dish and cook for 5 minutes.

Serves 4

25g/1oz/¹/₂ cup porcini mushrooms
200g/7oz/generous 1 cup bulgur wheat
750ml/1¹/₄ pints/3 cups hot chicken stock
15ml/1 tbsp olive oil
4 shallots, finely chopped
4 rashers (strips) back (lean) bacon, chopped
100g/3¹/₂oz baby spinach leaves, washed
6 baby plum tomatoes, halved
30ml/2 tbsp fresh flat leaf parsley, chopped
25g/1oz/2 tbsp butter
salt and ground black pepper

1 Place the porcini mushrooms in a small bowl. Pour over 150ml/¹/₄ pint/²/₃ cup boiling water to cover, and leave to stand for 15 minutes. Place the low rack in the oven and place a cast iron casserole dish on top of the rack.

5 Add the reserved liquor, the spinach, tomatoes, parsley and seasoning. Mix together. Cover and cook for a further 8–12 minutes, until the bulgur wheat is cooked and the risotto hot. Stir in the butter and adjust the seasoning to taste. Serve at once with salad or as an accompaniment to chicken dishes.

Energy 343kcal/1428kJ; Protein 11g; Carbohydrate 42g, of which sugars 3g; Fat 15g, of which saturates 5g; Cholesterol 28mg; Calcium 86mg; Fibre 2g; Sodium 844mg

Puy Lentils with Sausages

These small speckled lentils from France are considered to be the most superior. They cook quickly and do not lose their shape, and are absolutely delicious cooked with chunky pork sausages. This one-pot meal works very well in the halogen oven.

Serves 4

225g/8oz Puy lentils
1 onion, chopped
2 garlic cloves, crushed
750ml/1¼ pints/3 cups boiling
    vegetable stock
1 red (bell) pepper
2 rashers (strips) back (lean) bacon
375g/13oz pork sausages, cut into 4
5ml/1 tsp fresh thyme leaves
15ml/1 tbsp fresh parsley, chopped
salt and ground black pepper

1 Place the lentils in a pan with the onion, garlic and 450ml/¾ pint/scant 2 cups of the boiling vegetable stock. Bring to the boil, then reduce the heat and simmer for 20 minutes.

2 Cut the red pepper in half, remove the seeds and cut the flesh into strips; place in a cast iron casserole dish. Cut the bacon into strips and add with the sausage pieces to the pot.

3 Place the low rack in the oven and put the casserole dish on top of the rack.

4 Set the oven to 200°C/392°F and cook for 8–12 minutes, until the sausages have browned and the bacon is cooked. Stir once or twice during cooking. Remove the casserole dish from the oven, add the lentils, the remaining boiling stock and the thyme, and mix together.

5 Cover tightly with the lid, return to the oven, and cook for 12–15 minutes more, until the lentils are cooked, stirring half way through the cooking time.

6 Add the parsley, and check and adjust the seasoning. Serve immediately on warmed serving plates with French bread. Garlic bread is particularly good with this casserole.

Energy 447kcal/1877kJ; Protein 30g; Carbohydrate 38g, of which sugars 6g; Fat 21g, of which saturates 7g; Cholesterol 62mg; Calcium 191mg; Fibre 1.4g; Sodium 1220mg

Pork Burgers with Corn and Avocado Relish

With the halogen oven, you can cook the burgers and toast the buns at the same time, making this a stress-free meal. They are served with a tasty corn and avocado relish. For a special treat, serve them with fried potatoes.

Serves 4

400g/14oz minced (ground) pork
2 shallots, finely chopped
15ml/1 tbsp fresh parsley, chopped
45ml/3 tbsp fresh white breadcrumbs
1 egg yolk
plain (all-purpose) flour, for shaping
15ml/1 tbsp sunflower oil
½ red onion
4 sesame-seeded buns
salt and ground black pepper
lettuce and sliced tomatoes, to serve

For the relish:
1 ripe avocado
juice of 2 limes
½ red onion, finely chopped
195g/7oz can corn kernels, drained
30ml/2 tbsp fresh coriander (cilantro), chopped
30ml/2 tbsp olive oil
few drops of Tabasco sauce

1 In a large bowl, mix together the pork, shallots, parsley, breadcrumbs and egg yolk. Season well with salt and pepper. Divide the mixture evenly into 4, then with floured hands, shape into thick burgers.

> **Variation** You can make beef burgers if you prefer – just replace the minced pork with minced beef.

2 Place on an oiled baking tray. Cover and chill for 10 minutes. Place the low and high racks in the oven and preheat the oven to 200°C/392°F.

3 To make the relish, peel, stone (pit) and dice the avocado and place in a bowl with the lime juice. Mix in the red onion, corn, coriander and olive oil, and season with salt, pepper and Tabasco sauce.

4 Remove the burgers from the refrigerator and brush with sunflower oil.

5 Place the burgers on the high rack in the oven and cook for 9–14 minutes, turning over after 5–7 minutes, until the juices run clear.

6 Thinly slice the red onion while the burgers are cooking. Transfer the burgers to the low rack when cooked to keep warm, or remove from the oven and cover to keep warm.

7 Place the burger buns, cut-sides uppermost, on the high rack. Cook for 1–2 minutes, until toasted. Remove from the oven.

8 To serve, place lettuce leaves on the bases of the burger buns, top with tomato slices and a burger. Finish with sliced red onion and serve with the corn and avocado relish. Add some fried potatoes if you like.

Energy 501kcal/2103kJ; Protein 31g; Carbohydrate 50g, of which sugars 8g; Fat 21g, of which saturates 5g; Cholesterol 113mg; Calcium 122mg; Fibre 4.9g; Sodium 624mg

Stuffed Pork Fillet with Apples and Plums

This is a lovely dish to prepare when entertaining. You can stuff the pork fillet in advance, and just place it in the halogen oven to cook when required. The sharpness of the roasted plums and apples contrast superbly with the sweet flavour of the pork and feta cheese.

Serves 4

400g/14oz pork fillet (tenderloin)
75g/3oz feta cheese
30ml/2 tbsp fresh sage leaves, chopped
30ml/2 tbsp chopped fresh chives
4 rashers (strips) streaky (fatty) bacon
1 onion, cut into wedges
1 eating apple, cored and cut into
    wedges
30ml/2 tbsp sunflower oil
6 plums, halved and stoned (pitted)
10ml/2 tsp clear honey, mixed with
    10ml/2 tsp wholegrain mustard
ground black pepper
boiled rice, to serve

1 Place the low rack in the oven and preheat the oven to 210°C/415°F. Cut the pork fillet along its length without cutting right the way through. Open out flat and sprinkle with pepper.

2 Mix the feta cheese with the sage and chives, then spread this mixture along the pork fillet. Roll and close up the pork.

3 Wrap the bacon around the pork and tie the roll with string at 2.5cm/1in intervals. Wrap in foil, put in an ovenproof dish, and cook in the oven for 20 minutes.

4 Mix the onion and apple wedges with 15ml/1 tbsp of the sunflower oil in a bowl.

5 Remove the pork and take off the foil. Return the pork to the dish, upside down, and brush with the remaining oil. Reduce the oven to 200°C/392°F. Add the onions and apples to the dish, and cook for 15 minutes, turning after 7 minutes.

6 Add the plums and cook for a further 2–3 minutes, until tender. Drizzle over the honey and mustard mixture, and cook for 1–2 minutes more. Remove from the oven and cut the pork into thick slices. Serve, accompanied by the apples, plums and onions, with boiled rice.

Energy 388kcal/1617kJ; Protein 31g; Carbohydrate 14g, of which sugars 13g; Fat 23, of which saturates 8g; Cholesterol 94mg; Calcium 106mg; Fibre 3.1g; Sodium 663mg

Stuffed Squash with Spicy Minced Lamb

The flavouring for this lamb-stuffed squash is harissa, which is a Moroccan blend containing chillies, caraway, coriander and garlic. Butternut squash roasts well in the halogen oven, browning on top but still moist inside, and its sweet taste complements the spices.

Serves 2–4

1kg/2¼lb butternut squash, about
    23cm/9in long
15ml/1 tbsp sunflower oil
1 onion, chopped
350g/12oz minced (ground) lamb
3 tomatoes, chopped
20ml/4 tsp harissa
150ml/¼ pint/⅔ cup boiling vegetable
    stock
30ml/2 tbsp fresh white breadcrumbs
salt and ground black pepper
a tomato, basil and red onion salad,
    to serve

1 Place the low rack in the oven and preheat the oven to 200°C/392°F. Cut the squash in half lengthways and scoop out and discard the seeds. Scoop a channel along the thinner end of the squash so there is somewhere to put the stuffing.

2 Place the squash in a casserole dish, or round ovenproof dish, which will hold the two halves. Cook for 17–22 minutes, until the flesh is soft. If your oven browns quickly, use an extension ring.

3 Meanwhile, heat the sunflower oil in a frying pan, add the onion and sauté for 5 minutes, to soften.

4 Add the minced lamb and cook for 5–6 minutes, until browned. Stir in the tomatoes and harissa. Season to taste and cook for a further 2–3 minutes.

5 When soft, remove the lid from the oven and carefully spoon the spiced lamb mixture into the squash halves, dividing it evenly between the two.

6 Pour the boiling stock into the base of the casserole dish. Cover with foil and seal tightly so that it doesn't lift. Return to the oven for 10 minutes.

7 Remove the foil, sprinkle the top of the squash with breadcrumbs and cook for a further 2–3 minutes to brown. Serve with a tomato, basil and red onion salad.

Variation Try replacing the tomatoes with 30ml/1 tbsp each of pine nuts and raisins.

Energy 328kcal/1381kJ; Protein 22g; Carbohydrate 30g, of which sugars 16g; Fat 15g, of which saturates 5g; Cholesterol 67mg; Calcium 150mg; Fibre 1.7g; Sodium 339mg

Minted Lamb Kebabs

Succulent pieces of mint-flavoured lamb and red onion wedges threaded on to skewers are cooked in a matter of minutes in the halogen oven – much faster than cooking them on the barbecue and just as tasty. Make sure the skewers will fit in the oven.

2 Thread the marinated lamb pieces and onion wedges on to 4 metal skewers. Brush with any remaining marinade.

3 Place the low rack in the oven and put a shallow round baking tray on the rack. Place the high rack in the oven. Preheat the oven to 200°C/392°F. Mix the olive oil and remaining garlic together.

4 Place the kebabs on the high rack and cook for 5–10 minutes, turning over after 3–5 minutes (turn over when the tops start to brown). Transfer to the round baking tray on the low rack.

5 Put the French bread on the high rack and cook for 1–1½ minutes, until lightly toasted. Drizzle with a little of the garlic oil and cook for a further 1–2 minutes.

6 To serve, place 2 slices of French bread on each serving plate and top with a lamb skewer. Sprinkle with pepper and garnish with mint leaves. Drizzle over any remaining garlic oil. Serve at once.

Serves 4

400g/14oz leg of lamb or lamb leg
   steaks, trimmed of fat, and cut into
   bitesize pieces
30ml/2 tbsp sunflower oil
juice of 1 lemon
30ml/2 tbsp fresh mint leaves, chopped
15ml/1 tbsp ground coriander
2 garlic cloves, crushed
1 red onion, cut into wedges
45ml/3 tbsp olive oil
8 slices French bread
salt and ground black pepper
fresh mint leaves, to garnish

1 Place the lamb in a bowl. Add the sunflower oil, lemon juice, chopped mint, coriander, half of the garlic and seasoning, and mix together. Cover and leave to marinate in the refrigerator for 30 minutes, or up to 2 hours, if time allows.

Energy 357kcal/1480kJ; Protein 22g; Carbohydrate 6g, of which sugars 4g; Fat 27g, of which saturates 6g; Cholesterol 74mg; Calcium 57mg; Fibre 3g; Sodium 170mg

Lamb Steaks with Chilli and Coriander

Prepare these lamb steaks in advance, then all you have to do is just pop them in the halogen oven a few minutes before you want to eat. They can be marinated for up to 4 hours in advance, or even overnight – just cover and chill until you are ready to cook them.

Serves 4

1–2 fresh red chillies
45ml/3 tbsp fresh coriander (cilantro),
   finely chopped
1 spring onion (scallion), finely chopped
45ml/3 tbsp olive oil
15ml/1 tbsp lemon juice
4 lamb leg steaks, each about
   115g/4oz, trimmed
mashed potatoes, sugar snap peas and
   baby corn, to serve

1 Cut the chillies in half lengthways, remove the seeds and finely chop the flesh. Only use 1 chilli if you wish.

4 Place a round baking tray in the base of the oven to catch the meat juices and add the high rack. Preheat the oven to 220°C/392°F. Arrange the lamb steaks, spaced apart, on the rack.

5 Cook for 3–4 minutes, then turn the steaks over and cook for a further 2–4 minutes, until cooked to your liking. Increase the time if you prefer it well done.

6 Serve the lamb steaks on warmed serving plates, with mashed potatoes, sugar snap peas and baby corn.

Variation Roast some baby tomatoes on the vine at the same time, if you wish. Place between the lamb steaks for the last 2–3 minutes of the cooking time.

2 Place the chillies in a shallow dish, add the coriander, spring onion, olive oil and lemon juice, and mix together.

3 Add the lamb steaks to the dish, turning them over to make sure both sides are coated with the marinade. Cover and chill in the refrigerator for 30 minutes, or longer if time allows.

Energy 280kcal/1164kJ; Protein 23g; Carbohydrate 0g, of which sugars 0g; Fat 20g, of which saturates 0g; Cholesterol 85mg; Calcium 10mg; Fibre 0.1g; sodium 82mg

Roast Beef with Potatoes and Onions

Normally a meal reserved for Sunday lunch, this beef joint is so quick and simple to cook in the halogen oven you can easily make it for a midweek meal. Serve any leftover meat the next day with potatoes – baked or roasted in the halogen oven – and salad.

Serves 4

675g/1½lb topside of beef
30ml/2 tbsp sunflower oil
500g/1¼lb potatoes
1 onion
2 sprigs small tomatoes on the vine
salt and ground black pepper

1 Place the low rack in the oven and preheat the oven to 200°C/392°F. Place the beef on a shallow round baking tray and brush with a little sunflower oil. Season with salt and pepper. Place in the hot oven, and cook for 10 minutes.

3 Peel the onion and slice into wedges. Add these to the pan of potatoes, and pour over the remaining oil.

6 If the beef is now cooked to your liking, remove it from the oven, cover and leave to rest in a warm place on a serving plate.

7 Place the high rack in the oven and cook the tomatoes on the rack for 3–5 minutes while the potatoes and onions finish cooking. If the vegetables are already cooked, remove and keep warm while cooking the tomatoes.

4 Remove the oven lid, and add the oiled potatoes and onions to the baking tray, arranging them around the outside edge of the meat. Replace the lid and cook for 15 minutes.

5 Remove the lid of the oven again, and turn the beef, potatoes and onions over so that they brown on all sides. Replace the lid and cook for a further 10–20 minutes, until the potatoes are beginning to brown.

8 If you like beef well done, leave the joint in the oven and place the tomatoes on top of the onion and potatoes for the last 5 minutes of cooking time.

2 Meanwhile, peel the potatoes, and cut into four or six pieces, depending on their size. Place the potatoes in a pan of boiling water and parboil for 6 minutes, then drain and leave to dry for a few minutes so that the steam evaporates; this gives the potatoes a crisper finish when roasting.

Variation Replace the potatoes and onion with the same amount of parsnips and red onion if you wish. Use olive oil instead of sunflower, and for the last 5 minutes of cooking, add a garlic clove, thinly sliced.

9 Slice the beef, and serve on warmed plates, accompanied by the roast potatoes, onions and tomatoes, and with some horseradish sauce and gravy.

Cook's Tip Choose a joint of beef with a good layer of fat on top, as this will keep the meat tender.

Energy 373kcal/1569kJ; Protein 42g; Carbohydrate 25g, of which sugars 3g; Fat 12g, of which saturates 3g; Cholesterol 84mg; Calcium 27mg; Fibre 2.7g; Sodium 240mg

Cottage Pie

This family favourite is ideal for a midweek family meal in winter, served with a fresh green vegetable such as broccoli. To ensure the meat sauce cooks well, use a cast iron casserole dish; you can cook the pie in this, rather than transferring it to another dish, if you like.

Serves 3–4

15ml/1 tbsp sunflower oil
450g/1lb lean minced (ground) beef
1 onion, chopped
1 carrot, finely diced
30ml/2 tbsp plain (all-purpose) flour
15ml/1 tbsp tomato purée (paste)
400ml/14fl oz/1⅔ cups hot beef stock
675g/1½lb/3 large potatoes, peeled and
    cut into chunks
15g/½oz/1 tbsp butter
45ml/3 tbsp milk
salt and ground black pepper

1 Place the low rack in the oven and preheat the oven to 200°C/392°F.

2 Place the sunflower oil in a cast iron casserole dish and heat for 1 minute. Break up the minced beef with a fork and add to the casserole dish. Cook for 6 minutes, stirring after 3 minutes to break up the mince further.

3 Add the onion to the pot, then the carrots and mix together. Cook for 8–10 minutes, stirring with a fork halfway through. Remove the dish from the oven, stir in the flour, tomato purée, boiling stock and seasoning. Cover tightly with the casserole lid and return to the oven.

4 Cook for 20–30 minutes, until cooked and the sauce is thickened. Stir halfway through the cooking time.

5 Meanwhile, cook the potatoes in a pan of boiling, salted water for 20 minutes, until tender. Drain well, then mash with the butter and milk, salt and pepper.

6 Remove the casserole from the oven and transfer the meat to a 20cm/8in (1.5–1.75 litres/2½–3 pints/ 6¼–7½ cups capacity) round ovenproof dish. Cover with the mashed potato.

7 Place the dish in the oven and cook for 10–20 minutes, until the top is brown and the pie is heated through.

Energy 438kcal/1837kJ; Protein 30g; Carbohydrate 40g, of which sugars 6g; Fat 19g, of which saturates 7g; Cholesterol 72mg; Calcium 61mg; Fibre 4.1g; Sodium 509mg

Chilli Con Carne

This recipe shows you how to cook a classic chilli in the halogen oven. Make sure you break up the minced beef thoroughly before adding the boiling stock, and use a cast iron casserole dish as this holds the heat when you open the oven to add ingredients or stir.

Serves 4

30ml/2 tbsp sunflower oil
1 large onion, chopped
450g/1lb lean minced (ground) beef
1 celery stick, finely chopped
2.5–5ml/½–1 tsp hot chilli powder
30ml/2 tbsp tomato purée (paste)
300ml/½ pint/1¼ cups hot beef stock
400g/14oz can chopped tomatoes
400g/14oz can red kidney beans
salt and ground black pepper
tortilla chips and sour cream, to serve

1 Place a 20–23cm/8–9in cast iron casserole dish on the lower rack of the oven, and preheat to 225°C/437°F.

2 Add the sunflower oil and onion to the dish and cook for 8–10 minutes, until the onion starts to brown. Stir 2–3 times.

3 Break up the minced beef into pieces and add to the casserole with the celery. Stir together and cook for 8–10 minutes, stirring halfway through.

4 Add the chilli powder and the tomato purée, and cook for 1 minute more.

5 Add the hot stock and tomatoes to the casserole and stir to combine.

6 Cook for 3–5 minutes, until the sauce starts to bubble around the edges of the casserole. Reduce the oven temperature to 175°C/347°F and cook for a further 30 minutes, stirring twice during the cooking time to make sure the meat isn't over browning on the top.

7 Drain and rinse the kidney beans and mix into the chilli. Cook for 5 minutes more. Check and adjust the seasoning and add a little more chilli if you need to.

8 Serve the chilli at once with a large bowl of warmed tortilla chips and some sour cream.

Energy 378kcal/1582kJ; Protein 32g; Carbohydrate 22g, of which sugars 10g; Fat 19g, of which saturates 6g; Cholesterol 63mg; Calcium 97mg; Fibre 7.9g; Sodium 576mg

Beef Casserole with Herby Dumplings

A lovely warming winter casserole is hard to beat. Make sure you make this in a cast iron casserole dish with a tight-fitting lid so that the meat cooks and tenderizes without burning. It's easier to begin this dish on the stove, but it is then cooked slowly in the halogen oven.

Serves 4

45ml/3 tbsp sunflower oil
500g/1¼lb beef topside, trimmed of fat and diced
2 onions, chopped
3 carrots, cut into batons
2 celery sticks, diced
25g/1oz/¼ cup plain (all-purpose) flour
600ml/1 pint/2½ cups beef stock
150ml/5 fl oz/⅔ cup red wine
salt and ground black pepper

For the dumplings:
115g/4oz/1 cup self-raising (self-rising) flour
2.5ml/½ tsp baking powder
2.5ml/½ tsp mustard powder
50g/2oz/¼ cup butter or shredded suet (US chilled, grated shortening)
30ml/2 tbsp chopped fresh herbs such as parsley, sage and thyme
plain (all-purpose) flour, for shaping

Cook's Tip Most oven timers only run for 60 minutes, so you will need to re-set after 1 hour to continue.

1 Heat 30ml/2 tbsp of the sunflower oil in a 21–23cm/8½–9in cast iron casserole dish, add the meat and fry for about 5 minutes, until browned, turning the pieces so that they brown it on all sides. Remove the meat from the pot with a slotted spoon, to a plate, and set aside.

2 Add the remaining oil and onions to the casserole and sauté for 10 minutes, until beginning to brown.

3 Add the carrots and celery and cook for 2–3 minutes. Stir in the flour, then gradually stir in the stock and wine, and bring to the boil, stirring constantly.

4 Place the low rack in the oven and preheat the oven to 180°C/350°F. Meanwhile, return the meat to the casserole dish and season well with salt and pepper. Cover with the lid.

5 Cook in the oven for 1¾ hours, stirring after 1 hour, then again after a further 30 minutes.

6 Meanwhile, make the dumplings. Sift the self-raising flour and baking powder into a bowl, add the mustard powder and season with salt and pepper.

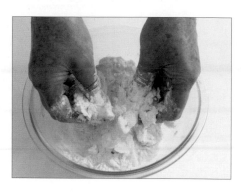

7 Rub in the butter until the mixture resemble fine breadcrumbs, or stir in the suet. Stir in the herbs.

8 Stir in about 60ml/4 tbsp cold water and use your hands to form the dough into a ball. Divide into 8 even pieces. Shape into balls with floured hands.

9 Remove the lid and place the dumplings on top of the casserole, half burying in the liquid. Re-cover and cook for 25–30 minutes more. When the dumplings are cooked, serve the casserole on warmed plates.

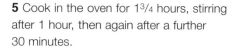

Energy 317kcal/1352kJ; Protein 31g; Carbohydrate 16g, of which sugars 9g; Fat 15g, of which saturates 3g; Cholesterol 63mg; Calcium 57mg; Fibre 3.2g; Sodium 47.6mg

Vegetarian and Vegetable Dishes

Vegetables aren't as obvious a choice for cooking in the halogen oven as meat and fish, because basically a halogen oven doesn't boil. It does, however, braise and roast very well, so there are plenty of vegetable dishes you can cook. These include beautifully roasted peppers, potatoes, parsnips and squash, as well as all your favourite vegetarian bakes, curries and casseroles. You will also find it easy to produce impressive vegetable tarts or delicious pre-cooked pasta dishes.

Red Lentil and Butternut Casserole

The sweetness of the baked butternut squash and spicy sauce combine beautifully with the red lentils in this recipe to make a warming and comforting meal. Serve with naan bread and chutney for a light lunch, or add a baked potato for a wholesome supper.

3 Meanwhile, heat the remaining oil in a large non-stick frying pan on the stove, add the onion, and cook for 5 minutes to soften. Add the garlic, ginger and chilli, and cook for 1 minute.

4 Rinse the lentils in a colander under cold running water and drain. Add the lentils, tomatoes, turmeric and coriander to the frying pan and mix together. Add the stock and bring to the boil. Transfer the squash to a casserole dish if necessary.

5 Pour the lentil mixture over the butternut squash in the oven, and stir to combine. Cook in the oven for 10 minutes, then remove the oven lid to stir again. Cover tightly with the casserole lid, or foil, and cook for 10–13 minutes more, until the lentils are cooked and the squash is tender.

6 Season well and serve immediately with warmed naan breads and chutney. For a more substantial meal, serve with baked potatoes or rice.

Serves 4

1 butternut squash, about 700g/1lb 9oz, peeled, cut into quarters, seeds removed
30ml/2 tbsp sunflower oil
1 onion, halved and sliced
1 garlic clove, crushed
2.5cm/1in piece fresh root ginger, peeled and grated
1 fresh red chilli, seeded and finely chopped
175g/6oz red lentils
4 tomatoes, roughly chopped
2.5ml/½ tsp ground turmeric
5ml/1 tsp ground coriander
600ml/1 pint/2½ cups vegetable stock
salt and ground black pepper
naan bread and chutney, to serve

1 Place the low rack in the oven and preheat to 200°C/392°F. Cut the peeled butternut squash into chunks.

2 Place the squash in an ovenproof dish or bowl. Drizzle over 15ml/1 tbsp of the sunflower oil and toss to coat. Cook for 10 minutes, stirring after 5 minutes.

Energy 300kcal/1270kJ; Protein 14g; Carbohydrate 45g, of which sugars 14g; Fat 9g, of which saturates 1g; Cholesterol 0mg; Calcium 127mg; Fibre 6.3g; Sodium 33mg

Baked Spinach Polenta

Polenta is a fine golden cornmeal that thickens when it is mixed with liquid and cooked. In this recipe, the thickened polenta is left to cool before it is sliced and baked with a spicy pepper and tomato topping and melted cheese. This is a great dish to prepare in advance.

Serves 4

150ml/¼ pint/⅔ cup dry white wine
300ml/½ pint/1¼ cups vegetable stock
115g/4oz/1 cup quick-cook polenta
50g/2oz baby spinach leaves
25g/1oz/2 tbsp butter
60ml/4 tbsp grated Parmesan cheese
1 egg yolk
2.5ml/½ tsp grated nutmeg
30ml/2 tbsp olive oil
1 onion, finely chopped
1 garlic clove, crushed
1 red (bell) pepper, seeded and chopped
1 fresh green chilli, seeded and
   chopped
2 tomatoes, chopped
5ml/1 tsp dried oregano
250g/9oz passata
50g/2oz/½ cup Cheddar cheese, grated
salt and ground black pepper
rocket (arugula) leaves, to serve

1 Line an 18cm/7in square shallow cake tin (pan) with clear film; set aside.

2 Heat the wine and stock in a pan until boiling, then sprinkle in the polenta, stirring constantly for 1 minute, until thick. Stir in the spinach and cook until wilted.

3 Remove from the heat and stir in the butter, Parmesan cheese and egg yolk. Season well with salt, pepper and grated nutmeg. Transfer to the prepared tin, spread out and leave to cool. When cold, cut into 8 even rectangles.

4 Place the low rack in the oven and put a cast iron gratin dish on the rack. Preheat the oven to 200°C/392°F.

5 Add 15ml/1 tbsp of the olive oil, the onion and garlic to the gratin dish and cook for 5 minutes. Add the red pepper and chilli. Return the dish to the oven. Cook for a further 8–10 minutes, until softened, stirring once or twice. Add the chopped tomatoes, oregano and passata, and cook for 2 minutes more.

6 Place the polenta rectangles in a shallow ovenproof dish and brush with the remaining oil. Place the high rack in the oven and place the dish with the polenta on top. Cook for 5–8 minutes.

7 Remove the polenta and sauce from the oven. Spoon the sauce over the rectangles and sprinkle with the Cheddar cheese. Cook for a further 2–4 minutes, until the cheese has melted and the polenta is hot. Serve with rocket leaves.

Energy 391kcal/1624kJ; Protein 18g; Carbohydrate 28g, of which sugars 6g; Fat 25g, of which saturates 11g; Cholesterol 90mg; Calcium 322mg; Fibre 4.2g; Sodium 560mg

Spinach and Ricotta Tart

This lovely tart is a perfect summer lunchtime dish when served with salad. It can be made in advance and served cold, so it would also be ideal for a picnic or alfresco eating. If time is short, you could use a ready-made 20cm/8in pastry case.

Serves 4

250g/9oz ready-made shortcrust pastry
30ml/2 tbsp sunflower oil
1 onion, chopped
1 garlic clove, crushed
125g/4¼oz baby spinach leaves
250g/9oz/generous 1 cup ricotta cheese
2 eggs
60ml/4 tbsp milk or single (light) cream
2.5ml/½ tsp grated nutmeg
50g/2oz feta cheese, crumbled
15ml/1 tbsp pine nuts
salt and ground black pepper

1 Roll out the pastry on a lightly floured surface and use it to line a 20cm/8in round fluted flan tin (pan). Prick the base with a fork. Line with greaseproof paper and fill with a layer of baking beans, then chill in the refrigerator for 10 minutes.

2 Place the low rack in the oven and preheat the oven to 170°C/340°F. Place the flan tin on a round baking tray and cook for 10–12 minutes. Remove the beans and paper, then return to the oven and cook the pastry case for a further 5–7 minutes, until pale golden.

3 Meanwhile, heat the sunflower oil in a large frying pan, add the onion and garlic, and cook, stirring, for 5 minutes. Add the spinach and cook for 2–3 minutes more, until wilted. Remove from the heat.

4 In a bowl, mix the ricotta, eggs, milk and nutmeg together with a whisk, then season well. Spoon the spinach mixture into the pastry case and pour the ricotta mixture evenly over the top.

5 Sprinkle with the feta cheese and pine nuts, and cook in the oven for 20–30 minutes, until set. If your oven browns quickly, you may need to add an extension ring so the top of the tart does not over-brown. Serve warm or cold.

Energy 592kcal/2463kJ; Protein 35g; Carbohydrate 35g, of which sugars 4g; Fat 44g, of which saturates 15g; Cholesterol 173mg; Calcium 343mg; Fibre 3.2g; Sodium 683mg

Roasted Italian Vegetables

The flavours of roasted vegetables always evoke memories of warm and sunny Mediterranean meals. This is a versatile dish, which can be served either as a side dish for meat and fish, or as a main vegetarian meal served with couscous or rice.

Serves 4 as a side dish or
  2 as a main course

1 aubergine (eggplant), about 250g/9oz
1 yellow (bell) pepper
1 onion, cut into wedges
30ml/2 tbsp olive oil
200g/7oz baby courgettes (zucchini),
  halved lengthways
400g/14oz can chickpeas in water,
  drained and rinsed
250g/9oz passata
30ml/2 tbsp fresh thyme leaves,
  chopped
salt and ground black pepper

1 Slice the aubergine widthways and cut each slice in half. Cut the yellow pepper in half, remove the seeds and cut the flesh into strips.

2 Place the low rack in the oven and preheat the oven to 200°C/392°F.

3 In a bowl, toss the aubergine slices and onion wedges together in half of the olive oil. In a separate bowl, toss the courgettes and yellow pepper strips together in the remaining oil.

4 Arrange the aubergines and onions on one round baking tray and place on the low rack of the halogen oven. Add the high rack.

5 Place the courgettes and peppers on another tray and place on the high rack of the oven. Cook for 10–12 minutes, stirring the top shelf of vegetables after 5 minutes, then swap the trays over and cook for a further 10–12 minutes, until the vegetables are tender. Stir the top tray of aubergines and onions after 5–6 minutes.

6 Transfer the roasted vegetables to a shallow cast iron gratin dish. Add the chickpeas, passata and thyme, and mix together. Return to the oven for 5–7 minutes, until the sauce is hot. Check and adjust the seasoning and serve immediately. Serve as an accompaniment or main course.

Energy 213kcal/897kJ; Protein 9g; Carbohydrate 53g, of which sugars 10g; Fat 10g, of which saturates 1g; Cholesterol 0mg; Calcium 82mg; Fibre 4.1g; Sodium 286mg

Vegetable Lasagne

A variation on the classic meat lasagne, this tasty pasta dish is made with roasted vegetables – aubergines, peppers, baby sweetcorn and mushrooms – combined in a tomato sauce and topped with a béchamel sauce and Cheddar cheese crust.

Serves 4

400g/14oz can chopped tomatoes
30ml/2 tbsp tomato purée (paste)
10ml/2 tsp dried oregano
1 aubergine (eggplant), about 225g/8oz,
   halved and sliced
1 onion, sliced
30ml/2 tbsp olive oil
1 green (bell) pepper, seeded and sliced
115g/4oz baby corn, each cut into 4
75g/3oz/12 medium mushrooms, sliced
6 large sheets fresh lasagne, about
   150g/5oz in total
salt and ground black pepper
fresh Greek basil leaves, to garnish

For the béchamel sauce:
450ml/³⁄₄ pint/scant 2 cups milk
½ onion
1 bay leaf
6 black peppercorns
40g/1½oz/3 tbsp butter
25g/1oz/¼ cup plain (all-purpose) flour
45ml/3 tbsp grated Cheddar cheese

1 Place the low rack in the oven and preheat the oven to 200°C/392°F. Place the tomatoes, tomato purée and oregano in a large pan. Add 150ml/¼ pint/ ²⁄₃ cup cold water. Set aside.

2 Heat the milk for the béchamel sauce in a small pan with the onion, bay leaf and peppercorns, then remove from the heat and leave to steep.

3 Toss the aubergine and onion slices in half of the olive oil, then spread over a round baking tray.

4 Toss the green pepper, corn pieces and mushrooms in the remaining oil and spread over a second baking tray. Season both trays with salt and pepper.

5 Place the green pepper tray on the low rack, add the high rack and place the aubergine and onion tray on this rack.

6 Cook for 10–12 minutes, stirring the top tray of vegetables after 5–6 minutes. Swap the trays over and cook for a further 8–10 minutes. Stir the top tray of vegetables after 5–6 minutes.

7 Meanwhile, make the béchamel sauce. Melt the butter in a pan, stir in the flour and cook for 1 minute. Remove from the heat. Strain the milk and slowly add to the butter and flour, stirring constantly. Return to the heat, bring to the boil, stirring, and simmer for 2 minutes.

8 Heat the tomato sauce until bubbling, then stir in the vegetables. Set aside. Cover the sheets of lasagne with boiling water. Leave for 1 minute, then drain.

9 To assemble, place one-third of the roasted vegetable and tomato mixture in the bottom of a 20cm/8in square ovenproof dish. Cover with 2 sheets of lasagne. Repeat twice, then top with the béchamel sauce.

10 Reduce the oven temperature to 190°C/375°F. Place the lasagne on the low rack in the oven. Add an extension ring if your oven browns quickly. Cook for 15–25 minutes, until hot, bubbling and cooked through.

11 Sprinkle with the grated cheese, then cook for a further 3–5 minutes, until melted and golden. Remove from the oven and leave to stand for 5 minutes, then sprinkle with basil leaves to garnish and serve with a green salad, if you wish.

Energy 459kcal/1925kJ; Protein 16g; Carbohydrate 50g, of which sugars 16g; Fat 23g, of which saturates 10g; Cholesterol 39mg; Calcium 288mg; Fibre 6.2g; Sodium 372mg

Stuffed Peppers with Goat's Cheese

These tasty roasted peppers are packed full of flavour. They are stuffed with onions, garlic, mushrooms and sweet cherry tomatoes, then topped with goat's cheese and pine nuts, and oven-baked. Peppers roast well in a halogen oven, charring slightly but remaining tender.

2 Place the peppers in the preheated halogen oven and cook for 7–10 minutes, until tender. Remove the peppers and leave the lid of the oven on its stand.

3 Meanwhile, heat the remaining oil in a frying pan, add the onion and fry for 4–5 minutes, until softened. Add the garlic and mushrooms, and fry for 2–3 minutes. Stir in the tomatoes. Remove from the heat and stir in the olives and a few thyme leaves. Season.

4 Turn the peppers over so that the cut sides are uppermost, then fill each pepper half with the vegetable mixture. Sprinkle over the pine nuts. Break the goat's cheese into small pieces and add this to the peppers.

Serves 4 as an appetizer or 2 as
  a main course

1 red (bell) pepper and 1 yellow (bell)
  pepper
30ml/2 tbsp olive oil
1 onion, chopped
1 garlic clove, crushed
50g/2oz button (white) mushrooms,
  sliced
8 cherry tomatoes, halved
25g/1oz/¼ cup pitted black olives
a few fresh thyme sprigs
25g/1oz/¼ cup pine nuts
75g/3oz soft goat's cheese
salt and ground black pepper

1 Place the low rack in the oven and preheat the oven to 200°C/392°F. Cut the peppers in half and scoop out the seeds. Place on a shallow dish, cut sides down, drizzle with olive oil and season well.

5 Return to the oven and cook for 3–4 minutes, until the cheese is golden. Serve the peppers garnished with the remaining thyme sprigs. Serve as an appetizer for four people, or as a main course with salad for two.

Energy 213kcal/884kJ; Protein 6g; Carbohydrate 10g, of which sugars 9g; Fat 17g, of which saturates 4g; Cholesterol 13mg; Calcium 94mg; Fibre 3.7g; Sodium 518mg

Coconut and Vegetable Curry

This is a Thai-style curry flavoured with coconut milk and red curry paste, which is now widely available in supermarkets. The vegetables can be varied to suit what is in season, just make sure the vegetables are not too chunky, so they will cook in the given time.

Serves 4

30ml/2 tbsp vegetable oil or ghee
1 onion, thinly sliced
2.5cm/1in fresh root ginger, peeled
   and grated
175g/6oz cauliflower florets
1 carrot, about 115g/4oz, cut into batons
175g/6oz/1 medium potato, peeled and
   cut into small chunks
175g/6oz young parsnips, cut into
   batons
175g/6oz green beans, cut in
   half widthways
30ml/2 tbsp Thai red curry paste
400ml/14fl oz/1⅔ cups coconut milk
300ml/½ pint/1¼ cups vegetable stock
salt and ground black pepper
15ml/1 tbsp fresh coriander (cilantro),
   chopped, to garnish

1 Heat the vegetable oil in a large non-stick frying pan, add the onion and cook for about 5 minutes, until softened.

2 Add the ginger, cauliflower, carrot batons, potato and parsnips, and cook for 5 minutes, stirring occasionally. Meanwhile, place the low rack in the oven and preheat the oven to 175°C/347°F.

Cook's Tip As the vegetables all cook together, make sure the ones that take the longest, like potato, are cut into the smallest pieces.

3 Add the green beans, curry paste, coconut milk and stock to the frying pan and mix together, then bring to the boil.

4 Transfer the mixture to a 23cm/9in ovenproof glass casserole dish, making sure the vegetables are immersed in the sauce. Cook in the oven for 30–40 minutes, stirring every 10 minutes. Test the vegetables after 30 minutes to see if they are tender. Check and adjust the seasoning to taste.

5 Either serve the curry straight from the casserole dish or transfer it to a warmed serving dish and garnish with the coriander. Serve with rice or naan bread and mango chutney.

Energy 226kcal/945kJ; Protein 6g; Carbohydrate 27g, of which sugars 14g; Fat 11g, of which saturates 1g, Cholesterol 0mg, Calcium 100mg, Fibre 0g, Sodium 527mg

Mixed Bean Casserole

This bean casserole, with a chilli and garlic kick, uses canned beans and is very easy in the halogen oven. You can vary the beans – perhaps try cannellini or butter beans, if you prefer.

Serves 4

30ml/2 tbsp olive oil
1 onion, finely chopped
2 celery sticks, sliced
1 garlic clove, crushed
1 fresh red chilli, seeded and chopped
2 fresh rosemary sprigs
500g/1¼lb passata
4 tomatoes, chopped
410g/14½oz can black-eyed beans
  (peas), drained and rinsed
410g/14½oz can red kidney beans,
  drained and rinsed
410g/14½oz can broad (fava) beans,
  drained and rinsed
30ml/2 tbsp fresh flat leaf parsley,
  chopped
salt and ground black pepper
sour cream, to serve

1 Place the low rack in the oven. Put a cast iron casserole dish on the rack and preheat the oven to 200°C/392°F.

2 Add the olive oil and onion to the hot casserole dish and cook for 5–8 minutes, until starting to brown, stirring once. Stir in the celery and cook for a further 2–3 minutes. Stir again.

3 Add the garlic and chilli, and cook for 2 minutes. Add the rosemary, passata, chopped tomatoes and 300ml/½ pint/ 1¼ cups boiling water, and cook for 10 minutes, until bubbling around the edges. Stir after 5 minutes.

4 Add all the canned beans and mix through the sauce. Cover the casserole tightly with the lid and cook for a further 15–25 minutes, until hot, stirring after 10 minutes.

5 Remove from the oven, stir in the parsley, then check and adjust the seasoning. Serve in warmed bowls, topped with sour cream and accompanied by rice or crusty bread.

Cook's Tip You can try adding other vegetables to this casserole, if you like. Try a red or green (bell) pepper, a leek, or some button (white) mushrooms, for example, rather than the celery.

Energy 319kcal/1349kJ; Protein 19g; Carbohydrate 43g, of which sugars 10g; Fat 9g, of which saturates 1g; Cholesterol 0mg; Calcium 136mg; Fibre 7.9g; Sodium 646mg

Pesto-Stuffed Mushrooms

Field mushrooms are the best mushrooms for this recipe, with a hollow that is large enough to stuff with lots of tasty filling. This dish is incredibly quick in the halogen oven.

Serves 4

6 slices fresh white bread, about
 150g/5oz in total
60ml/4 tbsp green pesto sauce
8 large field (portabello) mushrooms
30ml/2 tbsp olive oil
juice of 1 lemon
salt and ground black pepper
6–8 fresh basil leaves, to garnish

1 Remove the crusts from the bread and discard, then break the bread into pieces. Place in a food processor and process to make coarse breadcrumbs. Transfer to a bowl and stir in the pesto sauce, then season with salt and pepper. Set aside.

2 Trim the stalks from the mushrooms and discard. Brush the mushrooms on both sides with olive oil, then drizzle with lemon juice. Place in an ovenproof dish.

3 Place the low rack in the oven and preheat the oven to 200°C/392°F. Put the dish of mushrooms on the rack and cook for 5–7 minutes, until just tender.

4 Remove the dish from the oven and fill each mushroom with the pesto stuffing, dividing evenly. Return to the oven and cook for a further 3–5 minutes, until the crumbs have browned.

5 Serve at once in the baking dish, garnished with a few fresh basil leaves and a sprinkling of pepper. Serve as an accompaniment to meat or fish dishes. These stuffed mushrooms could also be served as a snack with crusty bread or a green salad.

Variation If you can't find large enough mushrooms, use smaller ones, remove the stalks, stand them closer together, cook for 4–6 minutes, then sprinkle the filling over the top rather than stuffing.

Energy 241kcal/1006kJ; Protein 8g; Carbohydrate 19g, of which sugars 1g; Fat 16g, of which saturates 3g; Cholesterol 6mg; Calcium 129mg; Fibre 3.2g; Sodium 362mg

Braised Spiced Red Cabbage

Red cabbage is a classic accompaniment to game dishes and is often eaten at Christmas time. However, braised red cabbage is so delicious it should be served throughout the winter months. Make sure the cabbage is finely shredded so the flavours of the ginger and spices permeate through and the cabbage becomes tender.

2 Finely shred the red cabbage, removing the central core. Add the cabbage and apple to the casserole dish and sauté for 5 minutes. Place the low rack in the oven and preheat the oven to 200°C/392°F.

3 Add the ginger, juniper berries, cinnamon, thyme, redcurrant jelly, stock and seasoning to the casserole dish. Stir well to combine and bring to the boil. Cover tightly with the lid and place in the preheated oven.

4 Cook for 10 minutes, stir, then reduce the oven temperature to 175°C/347°F. Cook for a further 30–40 minutes, until tender, stirring twice. Stir in the balsamic vinegar, then check and adjust the seasoning if necessary.

Serves 4

25g/1oz/2 tbsp butter
1 red onion, finely chopped
450g/1lb red cabbage
1 cooking apple, about 115g/4oz, peeled, cored and chopped
2.5cm/1in piece fresh root ginger, peeled and grated
5ml/1 tbsp juniper berries, crushed
1 cinnamon stick
2 fresh thyme sprigs
15ml/1 tbsp redcurrant jelly
300ml/½ pint/1¼ cups vegetable stock
30ml/2 tbsp balsamic vinegar
salt and ground black pepper

1 Melt half of the butter in a cast iron casserole dish on the stove. Add the onion and sauté for 5 minutes.

5 Transfer the braised cabbage to a warmed serving dish, discarding the cinnamon stick and thyme sprigs. Serve as an accompaniment to red meat, game or poultry.

Energy 85kcal/353kJ; Protein 2g; Carbohydrate 13g, of which sugars 11g; Fat 6g, of which saturates 3g; Cholesterol 13mg; Calcium 81mg; Fibre 4.7 g; Sodium 295mg

Potatoes Dauphinoise

This is a tasty French potato dish made from layers of sliced potatoes baked in a creamy garlic sauce and topped with melted cheese. It makes a good accompaniment for meat dishes – try serving it with a beef casserole or roast chicken – but it is also delicious as a meal in itself – served with a crisp green salad with a mustard dressing.

Serves 4

butter, for greasing
675g/1½lb/3 large floury potatoes
200ml/7fl oz/scant 1 cup double (heavy)
   cream
200ml/7fl oz/scant 1 cup milk
2 garlic cloves, crushed
75g/3oz Emmental or Gruyère cheese,
   grated
salt and ground black pepper
young fresh thyme sprigs, to garnish

1 Butter a 21–23cm/8½–9in round ovenproof dish. Peel the potatoes, then slice as thinly as possible. Layer the slices in the prepared dish, seasoning each layer with salt and black pepper.

2 Place the low rack in the oven and preheat the oven to 190°C/375°F.

3 Place the cream and milk in a pan with the garlic and bring gently to the boil. Remove from the heat.

Cook's Tip Make sure that the foil is well secured when using it to cover a dish, as the air movement from the fan of the oven could lift it and cause it to come off completely and cover the halogen heat source, which could be dangerous. Use an extension ring if your oven browns food quickly.

4 Pour the cream and milk mixture evenly over the potatoes, making sure they are just covered by the liquid. Cover the dish with foil, making sure it is tightly sealed.

5 Cook in the oven for 40 minutes, then uncover and cook for 20–30 minutes more, until the potatoes are just tender.

6 Remove the foil and sprinkle the cheese over the potato mixture. Cook for a further 5 minutes, until the cheese melts and becomes golden. Remove from the oven and leave to stand for 5 minutes. Sprinkle with young thyme sprigs to garnish, before serving the potatoes straight from the dish.

Energy 484kcal/2011kJ; Protein 11g; Carbohydrate 32g, of which sugars 4g; Fat 35g, of which saturates 22g; Cholesterol 93mg; Calcium 271mg; Fibre 2.7g; Sodium 276mg

Desserts and Baking

One of the most thrilling things about cooking in a halogen oven is watching cakes, puddings and breads as they rise beautifully through the glass bowl. Known mostly for its ability to grill and roast meat or fish, halogen ovens are not always thought of as perfect for baking – but they are. Achieve your best baking ever in record time, and conjure up tarts, cookies, bread rolls, cakes and puddings.

Apple Tarte Tatin

This wonderfully rich, buttery French apple tart just dissolves in your mouth as you eat it. Use slightly sharp eating apples to act as a foil for the caramelized buttery juices. Tarte tatin is sometimes thought of as a tricky recipe, but in the halogen oven it is really very easy.

Serves 4–6

100g/3½oz/½ cup caster (superfine) sugar
45ml/3 tbsp water
75g/3oz/6 tbsp butter
5 eating apples, peeled, cored, and cut in half
225g/8oz ready-made puff pastry
crème fraîche or Greek (US strained plain) yogurt, to serve

Variation You can also make tarte tatin with pears instead of apples.

1 Place the sugar and water in a pan and heat gently until the sugar dissolves. Bring to the boil and allow to bubble for 4–5 minutes until the solution becomes a rich brown caramel.

2 Pour the caramel evenly into the base of a shallow, heavy, flameproof 23cm/9in cake tin (pan). Dot with half of the butter.

3 Place the apples cut-side up into the tin, packed tightly together. Dot with the remaining butter. Place the tin on medium heat and cook for about 5 minutes to lightly cook and brown the apples.

4 Place the low rack in the oven and preheat the oven to 190°C/375°F. On a lightly floured surface, roll out the pastry to form a 24cm/9½in round; prick all over with a fork. Lift and place the pastry on top of the apples and tuck the edges of the pastry down the sides of the tin.

5 Cook in the oven for 15–20 minutes, until the pastry is well risen and golden. Remove from the oven and leave to stand for 10 minutes, then turn out on to a flat plate. Take care when turning out as the buttery juices will be hot. Serve the tart warm with some crème fraîche or Greek yogurt.

Energy 338kcal/1412kJ; Protein 3g; Carbohydrate 41g, of which sugars 28g; Fat 20g, of which saturates 7g; Cholesterol 27mg; Calcium 29mg; Fibre 2.5g; Sodium 195mg

Pear and Ginger Sponge Pudding

The spiced, poached pears add a lovely moist texture to this ginger sponge pudding.
They are kept succulent at the base of the dish until the pudding is served – turned
upside-down to reveal the sliced pears and stem ginger pieces.

Serves 4

2 pears
45ml/3 tbsp golden (light corn) syrup
50g/2oz stem ginger, plus 30ml/2 tbsp
   ginger syrup
115g/4oz/½ cup butter, cubed, at room
   temperature, plus extra for greasing
115g/4oz/½ cup light soft brown sugar
finely grated zest of 1 lemon
2 eggs, lightly beaten
175g/6oz/1½ cups self-raising (self-
   rising) flour
2.5ml/½ tsp bicarbonate of soda
10ml/2 tsp ground ginger

1 Peel, core, and halve the pears. Cut
each half into 4 slices. Simmer in a pan
with 30ml/2 tbsp water and the golden
syrup for 5 minutes. Add the stem ginger
and syrup, remove from the heat, drain
the pears and ginger, and retain the syrup.

2 In a bowl, beat the butter and sugar
together with a wooden spoon until light
and fluffy. Stir in the lemon zest.

3 Gradually beat the eggs into the
butter and sugar mixture. Sift the flour,
bicarbonate of soda and ground ginger
together and fold into the creamed
mixture. Place the low rack in the oven
and preheat the oven to 180°C/350°F.

4 Butter and base-line a 20cm/8in round
loose-bottomed springform cake tin (pan).
Arrange the pears in the base of the tin
and sprinkle over the stem ginger.

5 Spoon the creamed mixture into the tin,
spreading evenly to cover the pears
completely. Place in the hot oven and
cook for 5 minutes, add an extension
ring, then reduce the oven temperature
to 170°C/340°F. Cook for a further
25–35 minutes, until the pudding is risen
and firm to the touch. When done, a
skewer inserted into the centre should
come out clean.

6 Remove the pudding from the oven and
leave to cool for 5 minutes, then loosen
the sides of the sponge and remove the
cake tin edge. Place a plate on top of the
pudding, then invert the pudding on to
the plate, so the pears are now on top.

7 Remove the lining paper. Pour over a
little of the reserved syrup and serve
warm with cream or custard. Serve the
remaining ginger syrup separately.

Energy 574kcal/2412kJ; Protein 9g; Carbohydrate 79g, of which sugars 16g; Fat 28g, of which saturates 1g; Cholesterol 177mg; Calcium 206mg; Fibre 1.8g; Sodium 555mg

Bread and Butter Pudding

This bread and butter pudding, layered with pineapple, papaya, mango and melon, is an impressive dessert, but very easy to cook in the halogen oven. It is delicious served with lightly whipped cream or crème fraîche flavoured with ground cinnamon.

2 Place one third of the bread, buttered-side down, in the base of the prepared dish and sprinkle over half of the tropical fruits and sultanas. Cover with a layer of bread, buttered-side down. Scatter over the remaining fruits and cover with the remaining bread, buttered-side up.

3 Whisk the eggs and 50g/2oz/¼ cup caster sugar together in a bowl until pale and frothy. Gently heat the cream and milk in a pan until almost boiling, then whisk into the egg and sugar mixture. Stir in the vanilla extract.

4 Pour the cream mixture over the bread through a sieve (strainer). Press the bread down lightly. Set aside for 10 minutes.

5 Place the low rack in the oven and preheat the oven to 170°C/340°F. Sprinkle with the remaining sugar. Place the dish in a larger round baking dish.

6 Pour boiling water into the larger dish until halfway up the sides of the smaller dish to create a bain marie. Make sure no water goes into the pudding itself.

7 Cook for 30–40 minutes, until the custard is softly set and the top is crisp and golden. If your oven browns quickly, you may need to add an extension ring.

8 Remove from the oven, scatter with flaked almonds and serve warm, sprinkled with a little extra sugar, if desired.

Serves 4

50g/2oz/¼ cup butter, plus extra
  for greasing
8 slices good-quality white bread
75g/3oz soft dried fruit, such as mango,
  pineapple and papaya, chopped
50g/2oz sultanas (golden raisins)
3 eggs
65g/2½oz/⅜ cup caster (superfine) sugar
300ml/½ pint/1¼ cups single (light)
  cream
300ml/½ pint/1¼ cups milk
5ml/1 tsp vanilla extract
15ml/1 tbsp toasted flaked (sliced)
  almonds

1 Butter a 20cm/8in round shallow ovenproof dish. Remove and discard the crusts from the bread and butter the slices. Cut each slice into 4 triangles.

Energy 557kcal/2335kJ; Protein 16g; Carbohydrate 56g, of which sugars 22g; Fat 32g, of which saturates 17g; Cholesterol 242mg; Calcium 201mg; Fibre 6.2g; Sodium 541mg

Baked Cheesecake with Summer Fruits

This moist, vanilla-flavoured cheesecake topped with succulent summer fruits, such as strawberries, raspberries and redcurrants, is hard to beat. The cheesecake can be made a day in advance and kept chilled until just before serving.

Serves 6–8

75g/3oz/6 tbsp butter, plus extra for
  greasing
225g/8oz digestive biscuits (graham
  crackers), crushed
225g/8oz/1 cup ricotta cheese
225g/8oz/1 cup mascarpone
250g/9oz natural Greek (US strained
  plain) yogurt
3 large (US extra large) eggs
5ml/1 tsp vanilla extract
115g/4oz/generous ½ cup caster
  (superfine) sugar
15ml/1 tbsp cornflour (cornstarch)
450g/1lb fresh summer fruits
single (light) cream, to serve (optional)

1 Grease the base of a 23cm/9in round loose-bottomed springform cake tin (pan) and line with baking parchment. Place the low rack in the oven and preheat the oven to 160°C/325°F.

2 Melt the butter in a pan, then remove from the heat and stir in the crushed biscuits. Press the mixture evenly into the base of the prepared tin.

3 Place the ricotta, mascarpone, yogurt, eggs, vanilla and sugar in a large bowl. Sift in the cornflour and whisk together.

Cook's Tip Place the biscuits in a bag, and crush with a rolling pin.

4 Pour the mixture over the biscuit base and level the surface. Place on the low rack in the oven. Put the high rack in the oven and place a 7.5–10cm/3–4in metal disc from the base of a loose-bottomed individual tart tin (pan) on top, to deflect air movement from the fan.

5 Cook for 15 minutes, then remove the metal disc and cook the cheesecake for a further 15–20 minutes, until just set. You may need to add an extension ring if your oven browns quickly.

6 Switch off the oven and leave the cheesecake in the oven to cool for 10 minutes, then remove and leave to cool completely on a wire rack.

7 Once cool, chill in the refrigerator for at least an hour or until required. To serve, carefully remove the cheesecake from the tin and place on a serving plate. Top with a mound of fresh fruits, cutting in half first, if large. Serve on its own, or with single cream, if you wish.

Energy 507kcal/2115kJ; Protein 11g; Carbohydrate 42g, of which sugars 25g; Fat 34g, of which saturates 20g; Cholesterol 167mg; Calcium 190mg; Fibre 4.4g; Sodium 324mg

Lemon and Passion Fruit Tart

This is a twist on the traditional lemon tart. It still has a tangy lemon flavour but is laced with fresh passion fruit, which, along with the ground almonds, gives added texture.

Serves 4–6

225g/8oz ready-made shortcrust pastry
2 eggs, plus 1 egg yolk
125g/4¼oz/generous 1 cup icing
   (confectioners') sugar, plus extra
2 passion fruit, halved, insides scooped
   out with a teaspoon, skins discarded
finely grated zest of 1 lemon and the
   juice of 3 lemons
50g/2oz/¼ cup butter, melted
75g/3oz/¼ cup ground almonds

Cook's Tip If you can't find passion fruit, simply omit them.

1 Roll out the pastry on a lightly floured surface and use it to line a 20cm/8in round fluted tart tin (pan). Prick the base with a fork. Line with baking parchment and fill with a layer of baking beans, then chill in the refrigerator for 10 minutes.

2 Place the low rack in the oven and preheat the oven to 170°C/340°F. Place the flan tin on a round baking tray and cook for 10–12 minutes. Remove the beans and paper. Cook the pastry case for a further 5–7 minutes.

3 Meanwhile, whisk the eggs, egg yolk and icing sugar together in a bowl. Stir in the passion fruit pulp, together with the lemon zest and juice.

4 Stir in the melted butter and ground almonds, and pour evenly into the pastry case. Cook for 10 minutes, then reduce the oven temperature to 160°C/325°F. If the tart starts to brown in the first 5 minutes, reduce the oven temperature.

5 Cook for a further 8–12 minutes, until the filling is just set. Remove from the oven, and cool on a wire rack. Remove the tart from the tin on to a serving plate and dust with icing sugar before serving.

Cook's Tip In some models of halogen oven the fan is quite strong and the filling may swirl slightly in the centre before it has set. To deflect the air movement, add the high rack to the oven and on it place a 7.5–10cm/3–4in metal disc from the base of a loose-bottomed individual tart tin (pan). You can remove it after 10 minutes or so as the filling will have begun to set.

Energy 418kcal/1747kJ; Protein 7g; Carbohydrate 41g, of which sugars 23g; Fat 26g, of which saturates 9g; Cholesterol 95mg; Calcium 76mg; Fibre 2.5g; Sodium 222mg

Stuffed Baked Apples

This classic dessert of stuffed apples has a surprising filling of fresh blueberries, succulent dried apricots and chopped hazelnuts, and cooks very quickly in the halogen oven.

Serves 4

4 medium-size cooking apples
50g/2oz/½ cup fresh blueberries
25g/1oz/⅛ cup soft dried apricots, chopped
25g/1oz/¼ cup hazelnuts, chopped
30ml/2 tbsp dark brown sugar
2.5ml/½ tsp ground mixed (apple pie) spice
120ml/4fl oz/½ cup orange juice
25g/1oz/2 tbsp butter

1 Core the apples, then using a sharp knife, make a cut around the middle of each apple just through the skin, to help stop them collapsing during cooking.

2 Mix the blueberries, apricots, hazelnuts, dark brown sugar and mixed spice together. Place the low rack in the oven and preheat the oven to 190°C/375°F.

3 Spoon the fruit and nut mixture into the centres of the apples, pushing down to pack firmly. Place the apples in a shallow ovenproof dish, evenly spaced apart.

4 Pour 15ml/1 tbsp of the orange juice over each apple and top each one with a quarter of the butter. Cook the apples for 10 minutes. Pour over the remaining orange juice and add an extension ring if the apples are starting to brown.

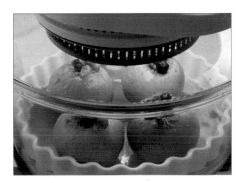

5 Cook for a further 5–15 minutes, until the apples are just soft. Baste after 10 minutes if you are still cooking the apples. Remove from the oven and leave to cool slightly, before serving with custard or vanilla ice cream.

Energy 205kcal/863kJ; Protein 2g; Carbohydrate 30g, of which sugars 30g; Fat 9g, of which saturates 4g; Cholesterol 13mg; Calcium 30mg; Fibre 5.8g; Sodium 46mg

Plum and Almond Sponge Flan

This is a classic French recipe that makes a mouthwatering dessert and is made with fresh plums studded through a moist buttery sponge and cooked in a pastry case. It is an impressive end to a meal, served warm with cream, or it can be eaten cold for afternoon tea.

Serves 4–6

For the pastry:
175g/6oz/1½ cups plain (all-purpose) flour
pinch of salt
75g/3oz/6 tbsp butter, chilled and diced
30–45ml/2–3 tbsp chilled water

For the filling:
75g/3oz/6 tbsp butter, at room temperature
130g/4½oz/scant ¾ cup caster (superfine) sugar
3 eggs
2.5ml/½ tsp almond extract
130g/4½oz/generous 1 cup ground almonds
30ml/2 tbsp plain (all-purpose) flour
60ml/4 tbsp plum jam
225g/8oz plums, halved, stoned (pitted)

1 Make the pastry. Mix the flour and salt together in a bowl. Add the chilled, diced butter and rub into the flour using your fingertips until the mixture resembles fine breadcrumbs. Add sufficient chilled water, a little at a time, until you have a firm dough.

2 Transfer the dough to a lightly floured surface and knead lightly for a few seconds to make a smooth dough. Wrap and chill for 30 minutes.

3 Place the low rack in the oven and preheat the oven to 170°C/340°F.

4 Remove the pastry from the refrigerator and roll it out on a lightly floured surface.

5 Line a 23cm/9in round loose-bottomed fluted tart tin (pan). Prick the base with a fork. Line with baking parchment and fill with a layer of baking beans, then chill in the refrigerator for 10 minutes.

6 Place the tart tin on a round baking tray and cook for 10–12 minutes. Remove the beans and paper. Cook the pastry case for a further 5–7 minutes, until light golden. Remove from the oven and cool for 5 minutes.

7 Meanwhile, make the filling. Beat the butter and sugar together in a bowl until pale and creamy. Beat in the eggs, one at a time, then beat in the almond extract. Fold in the ground almonds and flour.

8 Spread the jam over the base of the pastry case, then spoon the almond mixture over the top, spreading evenly.

9 Place the plums on top, cut side down. Return to the oven and cook for 15–20 minutes, until the filling is set and golden. Serve warm or cold.

Cook's Tip Always place the lid of the halogen oven on the rack when removing it to stir food or to remove it from the oven. The lid and halogen heat source will be hot, and could burn the work surface.

Energy 605kcal/2530kJ; Protein 12g; Carbohydrate 61g, of which sugars 35g; Fat 36g, of which saturates 15g; Cholesterol 169mg; Calcium 130mg; Fibre 5g; Sodium 270mg

Raspberry Crumble Cake

This is a delicious cake, which can be served either as a cake or for dessert with single cream or crème fraîche. The halogen oven crisps the hazelnut-flavoured topping perfectly.

3 Sift the flour, baking powder and cinnamon together, then fold a few tablespoons into the creamed mixture. Add the remaining flour mixture and mix in using your fingertips to form a crumb.

4 Place the low rack in the oven and preheat the oven to 175°C/347°F. Place half of the crumb mixture in the prepared tin and spread with the jam. Sprinkle over the raspberries.

5 Mix the remaining crumb mixture with the ground hazelnuts, then sprinkle this over the fruit. Place in the oven, adding an extension ring if your oven browns quickly. You may need to protect the top with foil towards the end of the cooking time. Cook for 30–40 minutes, until golden and firm to the touch.

6 Remove the cake from the oven and leave to cool on a wire rack. Once cool, carefully remove the cake from the tin. Serve warm, dusted with icing sugar and topped with a few fresh raspberries.

Serves 6–8

175g/6oz/¾ cup butter, at room temperature, plus extra for greasing
150g/5oz/¾ cup caster (superfine) sugar
1 egg, beaten
350g/12oz/3 cups plain (all-purpose) flour
7.5ml/1½ tsp baking powder
5ml/1 tsp ground cinnamon
350g/12oz/1¼ cups raspberry jam
75g/3oz/½ cup fresh raspberries, plus extra for serving
50g/2oz/½ cup ground hazelnuts
icing (confectioner's) sugar, for dusting
single (light) cream, to serve

1 In a large bowl, beat the butter and caster sugar together until creamy, then stir in the egg.

2 Grease a 23cm/9in round springform cake tin (pan) with butter and line the base with baking parchment.

Energy 554kcal/2331kJ; Protein 7g; Carbohydrate 85g, of which sugars 51g; Fat 23g, of which saturates 12g; Cholesterol 76mg; Calcium 93mg; Fibre 3.2g; Sodium 159mg

Double Chocolate Cookies

Homemade cookies are always a treat and these are no exception. The cookies will keep for several days in an airtight container, although they are unlikely to last that long!

Makes 8–12

50g/2oz plain (semisweet) chocolate
50g/2oz white chocolate
75g/3oz/⅜ cup caster (superfine) sugar
75g/3oz/6 tbsp butter, softened
2.5ml/½ tsp vanilla extract
15ml/1 tbsp milk
1 egg yolk
100g/3½oz/¾ cup plain (all-purpose)
    flour
2.5ml/½ tsp baking powder
50g/2oz/½ cup rolled oats

4 Spoon large teaspoons of the mixture into rounds on the prepared baking trays, 4–6 per tray, then flatten slightly. Cook one tray at a time for 7–12 minutes, until golden and slightly risen.

5 Remove from the oven and leave the cookies to cool for 5 minutes on the tray to firm up slightly. Meanwhile, cook the second tray of cookies. Transfer each batch of cookies to a wire rack to cool completely. Store in an airtight container.

Cook's Tip If you prefer, use chocolate chips instead of chocolate bars, then you will not have to chop the chocolate into pieces. Vary the flavours by using milk chocolate instead of the white chocolate, and add a little cinnamon if you wish.

1 Chop the chocolate into tiny pieces. Line 2–3 round baking trays with baking parchment or lightly grease. Place the low rack in the oven.

2 Place the sugar and butter in a bowl and beat until creamy. Add the vanilla extract, milk and egg yolk, and mix in.

3 Sift the flour and baking powder together and mix into the creamed mixture with the oats and chocolate. Preheat the oven to 160°C/325°F.

Energy 165kcal/694kJ; Protein 2g; Carbohydrate 21g, of which sugars 12g; Fat 9g, of which saturates 15g, Cholesterol 30mg; Calcium 34mg; Fibre 0.6g; Sodium 66mg

Banoffi Pecan Muffins

Freshly baked muffins are a delight to eat and these banana, fudge and pecan nut muffins are sure to please. Perfect for a weekend treat, they will disappear in front of your eyes.

Makes 6

175g/6oz/1½ cups plain (all-purpose) flour
7.5ml/1½ tsp baking powder
65g/2½oz/⅓ cup caster (superfine) sugar
1 banana
1 egg, lightly beaten
120ml/4fl oz/½ cup buttermilk
7.5ml/1½ tsp vanilla extract
40g/1½oz/3 tbsp butter, melted
40g/1½oz vanilla fudge, finely chopped
40g/1½oz/¼ cup pecan nuts, chopped
10ml/2 tsp demerara (raw) sugar

1 Line a 6-hole muffin tin (pan) with paper muffin cases. Place the low rack in the oven. Sift the flour and baking powder into a bowl and stir in the caster sugar.

2 Peel the banana and mash in a separate large bowl. Add the egg, buttermilk, vanilla extract and melted butter, and mix together. Preheat the oven to 175°C/347°F.

3 Lightly fold the flour into the banana mixture, then fold in the fudge pieces and three-quarters of the pecan nuts. Don't overmix or the muffins will be heavy.

4 Spoon the mixture into the muffin cases, dividing evenly, then sprinkle over the remaining nuts. Sprinkle with the demerara sugar. Cook for 11–15 minutes, until risen and firm to the touch. Use an extension ring if your oven browns quickly. Transfer the muffins to a wire rack and leave to cool slightly. Muffins are best eaten warm or within 24 hours.

Cook's Tip Use fudge chunks found in the cooking ingredients section of many supermarkets to save chopping the fudge pieces.

Energy 299kcal/1256kJ; Protein 5g; Carbohydrate 47g, of which sugars 24g; Fat 12g, of which saturates 5g; Cholesterol 18mg; Calcium 92mg; Fibre 1.6g; Sodium 181mg

Orange and Peach Drizzle Cake

This buttery Madeira-style cake, flavoured with orange zest and juice, and streaked with pieces of fresh peach, is finished with a drizzle of tangy orange-flavoured icing.

Serves 6–8

1 ripe peach, halved and stoned (pitted)
100g/3½oz/7 tbsp butter
100g/3½oz/½ cup caster (superfine)
   sugar
2.5ml/½ tsp vanilla extract
finely grated zest of 1 orange
2 eggs, lightly beaten
45ml/3 tbsp fresh orange juice
175g/6oz/1½ cups self-raising (self-
   rising) flour

For the icing:
10ml/2 tsp orange juice
40–50g/1½–2oz/⅓–½ cup icing
   (confectioner's) sugar

1 Grease and line the base and sides of a 450g/1lb loaf tin (pan). Cut the peach into small chunks. Set aside.

2 Place the butter and caster sugar in a bowl and beat together until pale and fluffy. Add the vanilla extract and orange zest. Gradually add the eggs and orange juice, beating well between each addition.

3 Place the low rack in the oven and preheat to 180°C/350°F. Fold the flour into the creamed mixture with a metal spoon, then fold in the chopped peach.

4 Spoon the cake mixture into the prepared tin and place on the low rack. Add the extension ring and cook for 10 minutes. Reduce the oven temperature to 160°C/325°F and cook for a further 25–30 minutes, until risen and firm to the touch. A skewer inserted into the centre should come out clean.

5 Remove the cake from the oven and cool in the tin for 15 minutes, then turn out on to a wire rack to cool completely.

6 For the icing, beat the orange juice and icing sugar together in a small bowl to make a smooth paste, then drizzle this over the cake. Leave to set. Store in an airtight container and eat within 2 days.

Energy 270kcal/1133kJ; Protein 4g; Carbohydrate 38g, of which sugars 21g; Fat 12g, of which saturates 7g; Cholesterol 85mg; Calcium 45mg; Fibre 1.1g; Sodium 100mg

Walnut Bread

Watching bread rise and turn golden is one of the great excitements of baking in a halogen oven. This tasty, rustic-style bread is delicious eaten with soft French cheese such as Brie, Camembert or Roquefort. The walnuts add a soft crunchy texture to the bread.

2 Knead the dough on a lightly floured surface for 10 minutes, until smooth and elastic. Place the dough in a lightly oiled bowl, cover with oiled clear film and leave to rise in a warm place for 1 hour, until doubled in size.

3 Turn the dough out on to a lightly floured surface and knock back (punch down). Shape into an oval loaf and place on a lightly oiled round baking tray.

4 Dust lightly with flour and cover with lightly oiled clear film. Leave to rise in a warm place for 30–45 minutes, until doubled in size. Place the low rack in the oven and preheat the oven to 190°C/375°F. Using a sharp knife, slash the top of the bread with three cuts.

Serves 4–6

350g/12oz/3 cups strong white bread flour, plus extra for dusting
5ml/1 tsp salt
7g/¼oz sachet active dried yeast
200ml/7fl oz/scant 1 cup lukewarm water
15ml/1 tbsp olive oil
50g/2oz/½ cup walnuts, roughly chopped

Cook's Tip Use an extension ring if your oven browns quickly.

1 Sift the flour and salt into a large bowl and stir in the yeast. Make a well in the centre, add the warm water and olive oil, and mix to a dough. Add the walnuts and knead into the dough.

5 Cook for 15–20 minutes, until the loaf sounds hollow when tapped on the base. Turn over for the last 5 minutes if the loaf starts to over-brown. Turn the loaf out on to a wire rack and leave to cool. Serve warm or cold, in slices.

Energy 281kcal/1184kJ; Protein 8g; Carbohydrate 44g, of which sugars 1g; Fat 9g, of which saturates 1g; Cholesterol 0mg; Calcium 91mg; Fibre 2.9g; Sodium 330mg

Potato and Parmesan Scones

These savoury scones make an interesting change from sweet scones. They are best served warm, straight from the halogen oven. They contain mashed potato, which makes them light and fluffy and keeps them moist during baking. Always preheat your oven when baking.

Makes 8

175g/6oz/1½ cups self-raising (self-rising) flour
5ml/1 tsp baking powder
2.5ml/½ tsp salt
5ml/1 tsp mustard powder
40g/1½oz/3 tbsp butter, diced
40g/1½oz/½ cup grated Parmesan cheese
75g/3oz/1 cup cold mashed potato
45–60ml/3–4 tbsp milk, plus extra for glazing

1 Sift the flour, baking powder, salt and mustard powder into a bowl. Add the butter and rub in until the mixture resembles fine breadcrumbs.

2 Place the low rack in the oven and preheat to 190°C/375°F. Add the Parmesan, mashed potato and sufficient milk to mix to a soft, light dough. Transfer to a lightly floured surface and roll out to about 2cm/¾in thickness. Cut into 8 rounds with a 6cm/2½in cutter.

3 Place the scones on a lightly oiled round baking tray, evenly spaced, and brush with milk.

4 Cook the scones in the hot oven for 7–10 minutes, until golden brown on the top and bottom, and cooked through.

5 Transfer the scones to a wire rack, then serve warm with butter. These scones taste delicious spread with butter and filled with smoked salmon and cucumber, or ham and sliced tomatoes.

Cook's Tip Use an extension ring if your oven browns quickly.

Energy 145kcal/609kJ; Protein 5g; Carbohydrate 19g, of which sugars1g; Fat 6g, of which saturates 4g; Cholesterol 16mg; Calcium 151mg; Fibre 1g; Sodium 474mg

Party Rolls

As the name suggests, these rolls are perfect for entertaining. You can serve the whole bread round and just pull off rolls as you want them. There is, of course, nothing to stop you cooking this bread for any occasion. Any leftover rolls can be frozen.

Serves 4–6

For the white rolls:
175g/6oz/1½ cups strong white bread
  flour
4ml/¾ tsp salt
5ml/1 tsp sugar
5ml/1 tsp active dried yeast
15g/½oz/1 tbsp butter
100ml/3½ fl oz/scant ½ cup lukewarm
  milk

For the granary rolls:
130g/4½oz/1⅛ cups strong Granary
  (whole-wheat) bread flour
50g/2oz/½ cup strong white bread flour
4ml/¾ tsp salt
5ml/1 tsp sugar
5ml/1 tsp active dried yeast
15g/½oz/1 tbsp butter
120ml/4fl oz/½ cup lukewarm water

For the topping:
1 egg yolk mixed with 15ml/1 tbsp
  cold water
15ml/1 tbsp poppy seeds
15ml/1 tbsp rolled oats

1 To make the white rolls, place the flour and salt in a large bowl and stir in the sugar and dried yeast.

2 Add the butter and rub in until the mixture resembles fine breadcrumbs. Make a well in the centre, add the milk and mix to a dough.

3 Knead the dough on a lightly floured surface for 10 minutes, until smooth and elastic. Place in a lightly oiled bowl, cover with oiled clear film and leave in a warm place for 1 hour, until doubled in size.

4 To make the granary rolls, follow the instructions for the white rolls but use the water instead of milk.

5 Turn both doughs out on to a lightly floured surface and knock back (punch down). Divide the white dough into 6 and the granary into 5. Shape each piece of dough into a small round ball.

Cook's Tip If the bread is not cooked all the way through, but is browned on the top, remove the side of the tin (pan), turn the bread over on to a shallow round baking tray and remove the base of the tin. Return the bread to the oven and cook for 5 minutes to crisp the base.

6 Lightly oil a 21–23cm/8½–9in round shallow loose-bottomed cake tin or springform tin (pan). Place 8 balls, evenly spaced apart, around the outer edge of the tin, alternating the dough. Place the remaining 3 balls in the centre.

7 Cover the tin with lightly oiled clear film and leave to rise in a warm place for 30–45 minutes, until doubled in size.

8 Place the low rack in the oven and preheat the oven to 190°C/375°F. Brush the rolls with the egg and water glaze. Sprinkle the white rolls with poppy seeds and the granary rolls with rolled oats.

9 Cook for 22–28 minutes, until golden. Use an extension ring if your oven browns quickly. When cooked, the bread should sound hollow when tapped on the base.

10 Remove the rolls from the oven and leave to cool in the tin for 5 minutes, then transfer to a wire rack to cool completely. Serve warm or cold.

Energy 142kcal/602kJ; Protein 5g; Carbohydrate 25g, of which sugars 1g; Fat 5g, of which saturates 2g; Cholesterol 39mg; Calcium 79mg; Fibre 1.3g; Sodium 281mg

Index